Sustaining Paradise

OrangeBooks Publication

1st Floor, Rajhans Arcade, Mall Road, Kohka, Bhilai, Chhattisgarh 490020

Website: **www.orangebooks.in**

© Copyright, 2024, Author

All rights reserved. No part of this book may be reproduced, stored in a retrieval system, or transmitted, in any form by any means, electronic, mechanical, magnetic, optical, chemical, manual, photocopying, recording or otherwise, without the prior written consent of its writer.

First Edition, 2024

ISBN: 978-93-5621-453-8

SUSTAINING PARADISE

SUSTAINABLE DEVELOPMENT IN SMALL ISLAND DEVELOPING STATES

DR. CHIRAG BHIMANI

OrangeBooks Publication
www.orangebooks.in

About Book

This book is not merely an academic exercise but a call to action—a call to prioritize the preservation of our planet's most vulnerable ecosystems and communities. It is a testament to the resilience and resourcefulness of SIDS and an acknowledgment of the collective responsibility we all bear in safeguarding their paradise for generations to come.

As we navigate the uncertain waters of the 21st century, let "Sustaining Paradise" serve as a compass, guiding us towards a future where sustainability is not just an aspiration but a reality—a reality where paradise endures, sustained by our collective efforts and unwavering commitment to a better world.

Dr. Chirag Bhimani

Index

About Book v
Foreword xiii
Preface xvii

Chapter - 1 1

Introduction to Small Island Developing States (SIDS) 3

1.1 Understanding SIDS 3

1.2 Unique Characteristics of SIDS 6

1.3 Challenges Faced by SIDS 10

1.4 Importance of Sustainable Development in SIDS 14

Chapter - 2 19

Historical Context of Sustainable Development in SIDS 21

2.1 Colonial Legacy and Its Impact 21

2.2 Early Environmental Awareness 25

2.3 International Recognition of SIDS Challenges 29

2.4 Milestones in Sustainable Development Efforts 34

Chapter – 3 41

Environmental Conservation and Biodiversity in SIDS 43

3.1 Fragile Ecosystems of SIDS 43

3.2 Threats to Biodiversity 47

3.3 Conservation Efforts and Success Stories 51

3.4 Integrating Traditional Knowledge with Modern Conservation Practices 54

Chapter – 4 61

Climate Change and Resilience Building in SIDS 63

4.1 Vulnerability to Climate Change 63

4.2 Adaptation Strategies 67

4.3 Mitigation Efforts 72

4.4 International Collaboration on Climate Change Resilience 76

Chapter – 5 81

Sustainable Energy and Renewable Resources 83

5.1 Energy Challenges in SIDS 83

5.2 Transitioning to Renewable Energy 87

5.3 Innovative Solutions in Energy Production and Distribution 92

5.4 Policy Frameworks for Sustainable Energy Development 97

Chapter – 6 103

Sustainable Tourism and Economic Diversification 105

6.1 Importance of Tourism in SIDS Economies. 105

6.2 Balancing Economic Growth with Environmental Preservation 109

6.3 Community-Based Tourism Initiatives 115

6.4 Promoting Cultural Heritage and Sustainable Tourism Practices 119

Chapter – 7 125

Ocean Conservation and Marine Resources Management 127

7.1 Blue Economy Opportunities 127

7.2 Overfishing and Sustainable Fisheries Management 133

7.3 Marine Protected Areas and Coral Reef Conservation 139

7.4 Harnessing Marine Resources Sustainably... 145

Chapter – 8 151

Sustainable Agriculture and Food Security 153

8.1 Challenges in Agricultural Production 153

8.2 Promoting Agroecological Practices 158

8.3 Addressing Food Security Concerns 164

8.4 Building Resilience in Agricultural Systems 169

Chapter – 9 177

Access to Clean Water and Sanitation 179
9.1 Water Scarcity Issues 179

9.2 Water Management Strategies...................... 184

9.3 Innovative Solutions for Clean Water Access... 188

9.4 Sanitation Infrastructure and Public Health.. 193

Chapter – 10 199

Governance, Policy, and Partnerships............201
10.1 Strengthening Institutional Capacity 201

10.2 Policy Frameworks for Sustainable Development... 205

10.3 Role of Civil Society and Community Engagement 211

10.4 International Cooperation and Partnerships 215

Chapter – 11 223

Education, Awareness, and Capacity Building 225
11.1 Importance of Education for Sustainable Development... 225

11.2 Raising Awareness on Environmental Issues 229

11.3 Building Local Capacity for Sustainable Development... 233

11.4 Integrating Sustainability into Curriculum and Training Programs 238

Chapter – 12 245

Conclusion and Future Perspectives 247

12.1 Achievements and Remaining Challenges . 247

12.2 The Role of Technology in Advancing Sustainable Development 253

12.3 Looking Ahead: Towards a Sustainable Future for SIDS 258

12.4 Call to Action: Empowering Communities and Stakeholders... 263

List of Acronyms..271
Glossary of Terms 275
Resources and Further Reading.....................281

Foreword

Forget the picture-perfect postcards and idyllic narratives. This book delves beyond the myth of "paradise" to explore the complex realities of Small Island Developing States (SIDS). We journey not to a utopian escape, but to a tapestry woven with breathtaking beauty, profound resilience, and the stark challenges of navigating a rapidly changing world.

The term "paradise" may paint SIDS with a brush of blissful ignorance, masking the intricate dance between humanity and the environment that unfolds on these islands. While many islands may include the classic swaying palms and turquoise waters, they overshadow the vulnerabilities that lie beneath the surface: socioeconomic challenges, rising sea levels, resource scarcity, and the ever-present threat of climate change.

SIDS represent the delicate balance between humanity and the environment. In "Sustaining Paradise: Sustainable Development in Small Island Developing States (SIDS)," we learn about the key challenges for sustainable development and the diversity of nations that fall under the SIDS umbrella. While these nations are vulnerable, they also are at the forefront of solving some of the most pressing issues in climate change and sustainable development. Nowhere is this commitment more crucial than in SIDS, where the convergence of limited resources, geographic vulnerabilities, and climate change threats creates a challenging landscape for development.

This book is a testament to the dedication of scholars, policymakers, activists, and community leaders who have tirelessly worked to address the complex issues facing SIDS. Through a blend of research, case studies, and personal narratives, "Sustaining Paradise" offers insights into the multifaceted dimensions of sustainable development in these regions.

Tackling critical issues for SIDS, rom the preservation of biodiversity-rich ecosystems to the promotion of renewable energy initiatives, each chapter delves into a key aspect of sustainability, highlighting both the progress made and the challenges that lie ahead. Importantly, the voices of those directly impacted by these issues resonate throughout these pages, reminding us of the human stories behind the statistics and policies.

As we navigate an era defined by unprecedented environmental changes and global interconnectedness, the lessons gleaned from SIDS reverberate far beyond their shores. They serve as beacons of hope, demonstrating that with innovation, collaboration, and a deep respect for nature, sustainable development is not only achievable but essential for our collective well-being.

"Sustaining Paradise" is more than just a book; it is a call to action–a call to forge a future where development is harmonized with nature, where prosperity is inclusive, and where the legacy we leave for future generations is one of stewardship and resilience.

I extend my deepest gratitude to the author for his invaluable insights and unwavering commitment to the cause of sustainability, putting island nations at the forefront.

Warmest regards,
James Ellsmoor
Chief Executive Officer
Island Innovation
(https://islandinnovation.co/)

Preface

"Sustaining Paradise: Sustainable Development in Small Island Developing States (SIDS)" explores the complex interplay between the unique environmental, social, and economic challenges faced by Small Island Developing States (SIDS) and the imperative for sustainable development. As the world grapples with pressing issues such as climate change, biodiversity loss, and socio-economic disparities, the plight of SIDS emerges as both a microcosm and a forefront of these global challenges.

This book delves into the multifaceted nature of sustainability in SIDS, offering a comprehensive examination of the strategies, policies, and initiatives crucial for safeguarding the fragile ecosystems and enhancing the resilience of these island nations. Through a blend of scholarly research, case studies, and expert insights, it endeavors to shed light on the intricate dynamics shaping the sustainable development discourse in SIDS contexts.

SIDS, despite their idyllic landscapes and rich cultural heritage, confront a myriad of vulnerabilities, ranging from susceptibility to natural disasters to limited resource endowments and geographic isolation. Moreover, the adverse impacts of climate change, exacerbated by rising sea levels, ocean acidification, and extreme weather events, pose existential threats to the very existence of these island nations.

In response to these challenges, SIDS have embarked on a journey towards sustainable development, seeking innovative solutions and forging partnerships at local, regional, and international levels. From adopting renewable energy technologies to implementing ecosystem-based adaptation strategies, SIDS are pioneering approaches that reconcile environmental conservation with socio-economic progress.

Yet, the road to sustainability is fraught with obstacles, including resource constraints, institutional capacity limitations, and external dependencies. As such, "Sustaining Paradise" underscores the importance of tailored interventions, tailored to the unique needs and circumstances of SIDS, while also emphasizing the significance of global solidarity and collaboration in achieving shared sustainability goals.

Dr. Chirag Bhimani

Chapter – 1

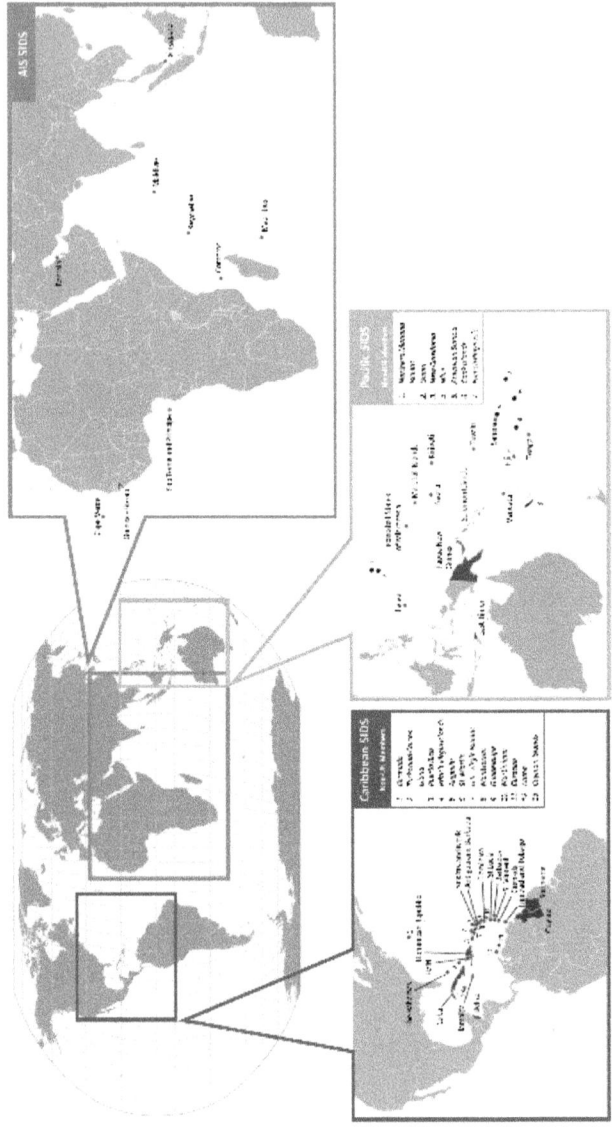

Introduction to Small Island Developing States (SIDS)

Small Island Developing States (SIDS) encompass a diverse group of nations spread across the world's oceans, facing unique challenges and opportunities due to their small size, geographical isolation, and vulnerability to external shocks. This chapter provides an overview of SIDS, their distinctive characteristics, the challenges they encounter, and the crucial role of sustainable development in securing their future.

1.1 Understanding SIDS

Small Island Developing States (SIDS) represent a diverse group of countries and territories facing unique challenges and opportunities due to their small size, geographic isolation, and vulnerability to external shocks. Understanding the distinctive characteristics and dynamics of SIDS is crucial for formulating effective policies, strategies, and interventions to support their sustainable development aspirations.

Geographic and Demographic Profile:

SIDS are scattered across the Caribbean, Pacific, Indian Ocean, and Mediterranean regions, encompassing a wide range of geographic features, from coral atolls and volcanic islands to larger land masses. Despite their diversity, SIDS share common characteristics, such as limited land area, narrow economic bases, and high population densities, which pose constraints and opportunities for development.

Economic Vulnerability:

SIDS face economic vulnerability due to their small size, limited resource endowment, and dependence on a few key sectors, such as tourism, fisheries, and agriculture. Their economies are often susceptible to external shocks, including natural disasters, commodity price fluctuations, and global economic downturns, which can disrupt livelihoods, undermine economic stability, and impede development progress.

Environmental Challenges:

SIDS are particularly vulnerable to environmental threats, including climate change, sea-level rise, extreme weather events, and environmental degradation. Their fragile ecosystems, such as coral reefs, mangroves, and coastal zones, are vital for biodiversity, food security, and coastal protection, but are increasingly threatened by human activities and climate-related impacts, posing risks to livelihoods and sustainable development.

Social and Cultural Dynamics:

SIDS exhibit rich cultural diversity, with indigenous peoples, ethnic minorities, and immigrant communities contributing to vibrant societies and traditions. However, social challenges, including poverty, inequality, health disparities, and youth unemployment, persist in many SIDS, undermining social cohesion, resilience, and well-being.

Governance and Institutional Capacity:

Effective governance and institutional capacity are critical for addressing the complex challenges facing SIDS. However, many SIDS struggle with governance deficits, including weak institutions, limited resources, and governance gaps, which hinder policy implementation, service delivery, and accountability.

International Relations and Cooperation:

SIDS engage in regional and international cooperation to address common challenges, advocate for their interests, and mobilize support for sustainable development initiatives. Through alliances such as the

Alliance of Small Island States (AOSIS) and regional organizations like the Pacific Islands Forum (PIF), SIDS amplify their voices, leverage collective action, and influence global agendas on issues such as climate change, ocean conservation, and sustainable development financing.

In summary, understanding SIDS requires recognition of their unique geographic, economic, environmental, social, and governance dynamics, as well as their aspirations for sustainable development and resilience in the face of evolving challenges and opportunities. By acknowledging these complexities and working collaboratively with SIDS, the global community can support their efforts to build inclusive, equitable, and sustainable futures for their people and environments.

1.2 Unique Characteristics of SIDS

Small Island Developing States (SIDS) possess a distinct set of characteristics that distinguish them from other countries and territories. These unique attributes, stemming from their small size, geographic isolation, and vulnerability, shape the socio-economic, environmental, and governance dynamics of SIDS and influence their development trajectories.

1. Small Size:
SIDS are characterized by their small land area and limited territorial extent, often comprising islands and archipelagos scattered across vast oceanic expanses. This compact geography presents both opportunities and challenges, influencing aspects such as resource management, infrastructure development, and urban planning.

2. Geographic Isolation:
SIDS are geographically isolated from continental landmasses, with many located thousands of kilometers away from major economic centers and markets. This isolation affects trade, transportation, and connectivity, leading to higher transportation costs, limited access to markets, and dependence on maritime and air links for connectivity.

3. Vulnerability to Natural Hazards:
SIDS are highly vulnerable to a range of natural hazards, including tropical cyclones, hurricanes, earthquakes, tsunamis, and volcanic eruptions, due to their location in disaster-prone regions. These hazards pose significant risks to lives, livelihoods, infrastructure, and ecosystems, necessitating robust disaster preparedness, response, and recovery mechanisms.

4. Exposure to Climate Change Impacts:

SIDS are disproportionately affected by climate change, experiencing rising sea levels, changing weather patterns, ocean acidification, and coral bleaching, among other impacts. These climate-related challenges threaten coastal communities, infrastructure, agriculture, fisheries, and biodiversity, exacerbating existing vulnerabilities and undermining sustainable development efforts.

5. Dependency on Key Economic Sectors:

SIDS often rely on a few key economic sectors for livelihoods and revenue generation, such as tourism, fisheries, agriculture, and remittances. However, the concentration of economic activities in these sectors can lead to vulnerabilities, such as overreliance on external markets, fluctuations in commodity prices, and vulnerability to external shocks.

6. Limited Resource Endowment:

SIDS typically have limited natural resources and face constraints in areas such as land availability, freshwater resources, arable land, and mineral deposits. This scarcity of resources necessitates prudent resource management, sustainable land use practices, and innovative approaches to maximize resource efficiency and resilience.

7. Cultural Diversity and Heritage:

SIDS boast rich cultural diversity, with indigenous peoples, ethnic minorities, and immigrant communities contributing to vibrant cultural landscapes and traditions. Cultural heritage, including language, music, dance, and art, plays a central role in identity formation, social cohesion, and community resilience in SIDS.

8. High Biodiversity and Unique Ecosystems:

SIDS are home to diverse and unique ecosystems, including coral reefs, mangroves, tropical forests, and endemic species, which contribute to biodiversity conservation, ecosystem services, and cultural identity. However, these ecosystems are increasingly threatened by human activities, climate change, and invasive species, requiring urgent conservation efforts.

9. Governance Challenges:

SIDS face governance challenges, including small administrative capacities, limited human and financial resources, and governance gaps, which can hinder policy formulation, implementation, and enforcement. Strengthening governance systems, enhancing transparency, and promoting accountability are essential for addressing these challenges and fostering sustainable development.

In summary, the unique characteristics of Small Island Developing States (SIDS) encompass their small size, geographic isolation, vulnerability to natural hazards and climate change, dependency on key economic sectors, limited resource endowment, cultural diversity, high biodiversity, and governance challenges. Understanding these distinctive attributes is essential for designing context-specific policies, strategies, and interventions to support the sustainable development and resilience of SIDS.

1.3 Challenges Faced by SIDS

Small Island Developing States (SIDS) confront a myriad of challenges that threaten their sustainable development, resilience, and well-being. These challenges, stemming from their unique characteristics, external vulnerabilities, and global trends, require concerted efforts and innovative solutions to address effectively.

1. Climate Change and Sea-Level Rise:

SIDS are among the most vulnerable countries to the impacts of climate change, including rising sea levels, extreme weather events, ocean acidification, and changing rainfall patterns. These phenomena pose significant risks to coastal communities, infrastructure, agriculture, fisheries, and ecosystems, exacerbating existing vulnerabilities and undermining sustainable development efforts.

2. Natural Disasters and Environmental Hazards:

SIDS are exposed to a range of natural hazards, including tropical cyclones, hurricanes, earthquakes, tsunamis, volcanic eruptions, and coastal erosion, due to their location in disaster-prone regions. These hazards can cause loss of life, displacement, damage to infrastructure, disruptions to essential services, and long-term socio-economic impacts, requiring robust disaster preparedness, response, and recovery measures.

3. Vulnerability of Key Economic Sectors:

SIDS rely heavily on a few key economic sectors, such as tourism, fisheries, agriculture, and remittances, which are vulnerable to external shocks, including economic downturns, natural disasters, climate change impacts, and global crises such as the COVID-19 pandemic. Fluctuations in these sectors can have ripple effects on employment, income generation, government revenues, and social stability in SIDS.

4. Limited Access to Finance and Investment:

SIDS face challenges in accessing affordable finance and investment for sustainable development initiatives, due to factors such as small economies, limited domestic savings, high debt levels, and perceived investment risks. This constrains their ability to finance infrastructure projects, renewable energy transitions, climate adaptation measures, and social programs, hindering their development aspirations.

5. Environmental Degradation and Biodiversity Loss:

SIDS grapple with environmental degradation, including deforestation, soil erosion, pollution, habitat destruction, and loss of biodiversity, driven by unsustainable land use practices, urbanization, industrialization, and inadequate waste management. These environmental pressures degrade ecosystems, compromise ecosystem services, threaten food security, and undermine resilience to climate change impacts.

6. Water Scarcity and Quality:

SIDS face challenges related to water scarcity, inadequate access to safe drinking water, and poor water quality, exacerbated by factors such as limited freshwater resources, population growth, urbanization, pollution, and climate variability. Water scarcity affects agriculture, industry, public health, and ecosystem health, necessitating sustainable water management practices and investments in water infrastructure.

7. Energy Dependency and Affordability:

SIDS are often dependent on imported fossil fuels for energy generation, leading to high energy costs, vulnerability to price fluctuations, and environmental impacts associated with fossil fuel combustion. Transitioning to renewable energy sources, improving energy efficiency, and enhancing energy access are critical for reducing energy dependency, enhancing energy security, and mitigating climate change impacts in SIDS.

8. Governance and Institutional Capacity:

SIDS face governance challenges, including limited institutional capacity, weak regulatory frameworks, corruption, and governance gaps, which hinder policy formulation, implementation, and enforcement. Strengthening governance systems, enhancing transparency, accountability, and participation, and building institutional resilience are essential for addressing these challenges and fostering sustainable development in SIDS.

In summary, Small Island Developing States (SIDS) confront multifaceted challenges related to climate change, natural disasters, economic vulnerability, environmental degradation, water scarcity, energy dependency, and governance deficits. Addressing these challenges requires integrated, context-specific approaches, international cooperation, and sustainable development strategies tailored to the unique needs and circumstances of SIDS.

1.4 Importance of Sustainable Development in SIDS

Sustainable development is paramount for the long-term prosperity, resilience, and well-being of Small Island Developing States (SIDS). Recognizing the intrinsic linkages between economic, social, and environmental dimensions, SIDS prioritize sustainable development as a pathway to achieving inclusive, equitable, and resilient societies. This section delves into the significance of sustainable development in SIDS and the key principles that underpin their development aspirations.

1. Promoting Resilience and Adaptation:

Sustainable development fosters resilience and adaptation to the unique challenges facing SIDS, including climate change impacts, natural disasters, and environmental degradation. By integrating resilience-building measures into development planning, infrastructure investments, and policy frameworks, SIDS can enhance their capacity to withstand shocks and recover swiftly from adverse events, safeguarding lives, livelihoods, and ecosystems.

2. Safeguarding Environmental Resources:

Sustainable development prioritizes the conservation and sustainable use of natural resources, including biodiversity, water, land, and marine ecosystems, which are vital for the socio-economic well-being of SIDS. By adopting sustainable land management practices, protecting fragile ecosystems, and promoting biodiversity conservation, SIDS can preserve their natural heritage, maintain ecosystem services, and support sustainable livelihoods for future generations.

3. Fostering Economic Diversification and Stability:

Sustainable development promotes economic diversification, innovation, and entrepreneurship, reducing SIDS' dependence on a few key sectors and enhancing their resilience to external shocks. By investing in renewable energy, sustainable tourism, eco-friendly agriculture, and green technologies, SIDS can unlock new economic opportunities, create jobs, stimulate growth, and build more inclusive and resilient economies.

4. Enhancing Social Inclusion and Equity:

Sustainable development prioritizes social inclusion, equity, and human rights, ensuring that development benefits reach all segments of society, including marginalized groups, indigenous peoples, and vulnerable populations. By addressing poverty, inequality, and social disparities through inclusive policies, social protection programs, and participatory approaches, SIDS can promote social cohesion, empower communities, and advance human development outcomes.

5. Strengthening Governance and Institutional Capacity:

Sustainable development emphasizes good governance, transparency, accountability, and institutional resilience as essential enablers for effective policy implementation, decision-making, and service delivery in SIDS. By strengthening governance systems, combating corruption, and promoting citizen participation, SIDS can build trust, legitimacy, and public confidence in institutions, fostering an enabling environment for sustainable development.

6. Fostering International Cooperation and Partnerships:

Sustainable development encourages international cooperation, solidarity, and partnerships to address common challenges, mobilize resources, and share knowledge and best practices among SIDS and the global community. By leveraging South-South cooperation, multilateral partnerships, and development assistance, SIDS can access technical expertise, financial resources, and capacity-building support to implement sustainable development initiatives and achieve shared goals.

In conclusion, sustainable development is essential for advancing the prosperity, resilience, and sustainability of Small Island Developing States (SIDS). By embracing the principles of sustainability and integrating them into development strategies, policies, and actions, SIDS can chart a course towards a more prosperous, inclusive, and resilient future for their people and environments.

Classification of small island types

Continental islands

Physical:
- >80% continental rock
- Usually (but not always) adjacent to a large landmass
- Typically larger
- Diverse topography (can be high or low)
- Subject to higher storm surge because of slope bathymetry

Human Exposure:
- Rich diversity of soils and vegetation
- Often more resources (as larger and near mainland)
- Inhabitants can sometimes migrate to the mainland

Volcanic islands

Physical:
- >80% igneous rock
- Sometimes volcanically active or recently extinct
- Worldwide distribution
- Typically high and distant from larger landmasses
- Fertile soils, often high rainfall
- Limited fringing coral reefs

Human Exposure:
- Prone to landslides and flash flooding
- Settlements around the coast (coastal squeeze)
- Inhabitants can sometimes move up-slope

Reef islands/atolls

Physical:
- >80% calcareous rock, reef and unconsolidated sediments
- Typically low and flat
- Often with well developed coral reefs (atolls)
- Poorer soils

Human Exposure:
- Settlements subject to coastal inundation by king tides
- Surface water limited
- Often hard sea defences are necessary (expensive)
- Land reclamation to accommodate growing populations

Raised limestone islands

Physical:
- >80% calcareous rock, often reef-associated
- Commonest in those places where (tectonic) uplift has been occurring
- Can be high or low
- Often steep sided but flat topped
- Lack of surface water

Human Exposure:
- Need for collection and storage of water
- Poor soils (flood insecurity)
- Inhabitants can sometimes move up-slope or inland

Composite islands

Physical:
- <80 % volcanic and <80 % limestone rock
- Typically formed by alternating volcanism and uplift
- Diverse topography
- Can be high or low
- Lack of surface water

Human Exposure:
- Rich diversity of soils and vegetation
- Inhabitants can sometimes move up-slope or inland

Chapter – 2

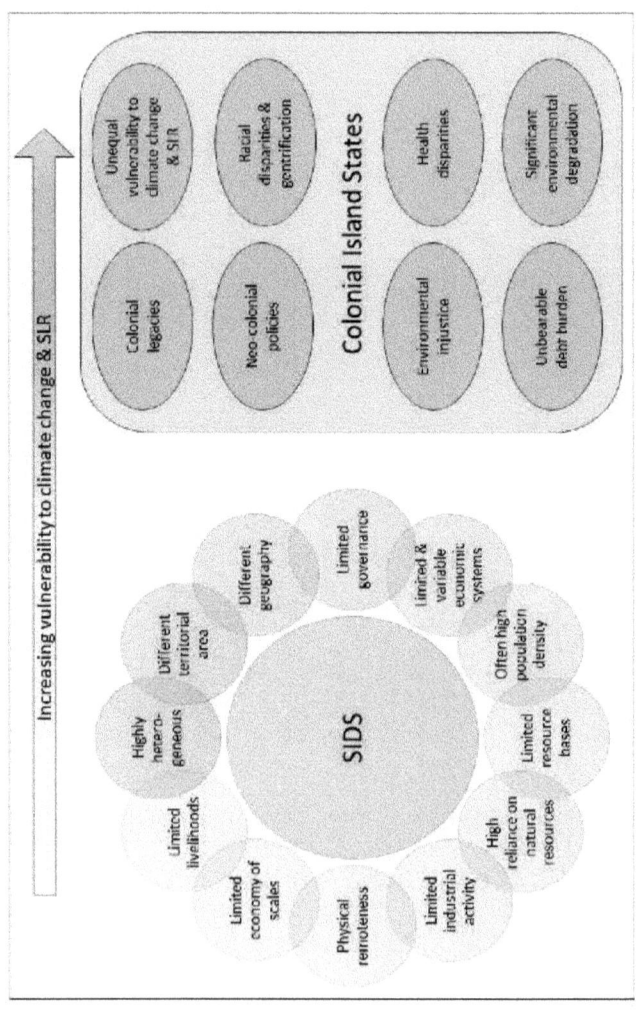

Historical Context of Sustainable Development in SIDS

Sustainable development in Small Island Developing States (SIDS) is shaped by a complex historical context marked by colonial legacies, early environmental awareness, international recognition of challenges, and significant milestones in sustainable development efforts. This chapter delves into the historical evolution of sustainable development in SIDS, highlighting key factors and events that have influenced their trajectory.

2.1 Colonial Legacy and Its Impact

The colonial legacy has left an indelible mark on the socio-economic, political, and cultural landscapes of Small Island Developing States (SIDS). This section explores the historical context of colonization in SIDS, the legacies it has bequeathed, and its enduring impact on contemporary development challenges and opportunities.

Colonial Expansion in SIDS:

During the Age of Exploration and European colonization, many SIDS became territories of European powers, including Britain, France, Spain, the Netherlands, and Portugal. Colonial powers exploited SIDS for their strategic location, natural resources, and labor, reshaping their societies, economies, and governance structures to serve imperial interests.

Economic Exploitation and Dependence:

Colonial regimes imposed extractive economic systems in SIDS, exploiting natural resources, such as sugar, spices, minerals, and timber, for export to the metropole. Plantation agriculture, slave labor, and monoculture crops dominated the economy, leading to dependency, inequality, and environmental degradation in SIDS.

Social Disruption and Cultural Erosion:

Colonization disrupted indigenous societies and cultures in SIDS, leading to forced displacement, cultural assimilation, and loss of traditional knowledge and practices. Indigenous peoples were subjected to oppression, marginalization, and discrimination, eroding their social cohesion, identity, and autonomy.

Institutional Imposition and Governance Structures:

Colonial powers imposed centralized governance structures, legal systems, and administrative frameworks in SIDS, often overlooking indigenous governance systems and traditional authorities. This legacy of colonial governance has persisted in post-independence SIDS, contributing to governance deficits, institutional fragility, and challenges in decision-making and service delivery.

Infrastructure Development and Urbanization:

Colonial administrations invested in infrastructure development, including ports, roads, and urban centers, to facilitate trade and administration in SIDS. However, these investments were often skewed towards colonial interests, neglecting rural areas, indigenous communities, and basic services, exacerbating spatial inequalities and urban-rural disparities.

Environmental Degradation and Resource Extraction:

Colonial exploitation of natural resources in SIDS led to environmental degradation, deforestation, soil erosion, and loss of biodiversity. The legacy of resource extraction continues to shape land use patterns, resource management practices, and environmental challenges in SIDS, underscoring the need for sustainable development approaches.

Legacy of Inequality and Social Injustice:

The colonial legacy has perpetuated inequalities, social injustices, and power imbalances in SIDS, manifested in disparities in wealth, land ownership, education, and access to opportunities. Addressing historical injustices and promoting social equity are central to advancing sustainable development and reconciliation in SIDS.

Resilience and Cultural Survival:

Despite the profound impacts of colonization, indigenous peoples in SIDS have demonstrated resilience, cultural survival, and resistance to assimilation. Indigenous knowledge, languages, and cultural practices continue to play a vital role in identity formation, community resilience, and sustainable development initiatives in SIDS.

In summary, the colonial legacy has left a complex and enduring impact on Small Island Developing States, shaping their socio-economic structures, governance systems, environmental landscapes, and cultural identities. Understanding this legacy is essential for addressing historical injustices, promoting reconciliation, and advancing sustainable development in SIDS.

2.2 Early Environmental Awareness

Amidst growing environmental concerns globally, SIDS began to recognize the importance of preserving their natural heritage and traditional knowledge systems. Indigenous communities and local leaders played pivotal roles in raising awareness about the value of ecosystems, biodiversity, and sustainable resource management practices. Efforts to protect fragile environments, such as establishing nature reserves and promoting traditional conservation practices, laid the foundation for future sustainable development initiatives.

In Small Island Developing States (SIDS), early environmental awareness emerged as a response to the profound ecological changes wrought by colonialism and rapid economic development. This section explores the evolution of environmental consciousness in SIDS, tracing its roots in indigenous knowledge, cultural traditions, and historical experiences, and its significance in shaping contemporary environmental policies and practices.

Indigenous Wisdom and Traditional Ecological Knowledge:

Indigenous peoples in SIDS have long maintained intricate relationships with their natural environments, grounded in traditional ecological knowledge passed down through generations. This wisdom encompasses sustainable resource management practices, conservation ethics, and spiritual connections to the land and sea, providing valuable insights into ecosystem dynamics and resilience.

Cultural Practices and Resource Stewardship:

Cultural traditions and practices in SIDS often embody principles of environmental stewardship and sustainability. From customary land tenure systems to traditional fishing methods, cultural norms have fostered respect for natural resources, communal cooperation, and adaptive responses to environmental change, laying the groundwork for early environmental consciousness.

Colonial Encounters and Environmental Impact:

Colonization in SIDS brought profound environmental changes, including deforestation, soil erosion, habitat destruction, and pollution, driven by extractive industries and plantation agriculture. Indigenous communities witnessed the degradation of their ancestral lands and waters, spurring resistance movements, advocacy for land rights, and calls for environmental protection.

Early Conservation Efforts and Advocacy:

In response to environmental degradation, early conservation efforts emerged in SIDS, led by indigenous leaders, community activists, and environmental advocates. These grassroots movements championed causes such as forest preservation, marine conservation, and cultural heritage protection, raising awareness, mobilizing support, and influencing policy agendas.

Scientific Exploration and Environmental Research:

Scientific exploration and environmental research played a pivotal role in documenting the ecological diversity and fragility of SIDS, raising awareness about environmental challenges and informing conservation strategies. Researchers and naturalists conducted studies on biodiversity, ecosystem dynamics, and climate variability, highlighting the importance of preserving SIDS' natural heritage.

Global Environmental Movements and Solidarity:

SIDS became active participants in global environmental movements, forging alliances with international organizations, environmental NGOs, and civil society groups. Through platforms such as the United Nations Conference on the Human Environment (Stockholm, 1972) and the Earth Summit (Rio de Janeiro, 1992), SIDS advocated for sustainable development principles, environmental justice, and climate action.

Policy Responses and Environmental Governance:

Early environmental awareness catalyzed policy responses and institutional reforms in SIDS, leading to the establishment of protected areas, environmental regulations, and sustainable development plans. Governments recognized the importance of integrating environmental considerations into decision-making processes, fostering inter-sectoral coordination, and promoting community engagement in environmental governance.

Education and Public Awareness:

Education and public awareness campaigns played a critical role in promoting environmental consciousness and behavior change in SIDS. Schools, community organizations, and media outlets disseminated information about environmental issues, sustainable lifestyles, and conservation practices, empowering individuals and communities to take action for environmental stewardship.

In summary, early environmental awareness in Small Island Developing States (SIDS) emerged as a response to colonial exploitation, cultural traditions, and global environmental movements, shaping conservation efforts, policy responses, and public attitudes towards environmental stewardship. Building on this legacy, SIDS continue to prioritize environmental sustainability, resilience, and community-led conservation initiatives in their quest for sustainable development.

2.3 International Recognition of SIDS Challenges

The unique vulnerabilities and development challenges faced by SIDS gained international recognition in the latter half of the 20th century. Forums such as the United Nations Conference on the Human Environment (Stockholm, 1972) and the World Conference on Environment and Development (Rio de Janeiro, 1992) provided platforms for SIDS to voice their concerns and advocate for sustainable development principles. The Barbados Programme of Action (1994) and the Mauritius Strategy for the Further Implementation of the Programme of Action for the Sustainable Development of SIDS (2005) underscored the special needs and circumstances of SIDS, leading to increased attention and support from the international community.

Small Island Developing States (SIDS) have gained international recognition for their unique vulnerabilities and development challenges, leading to concerted efforts by the global community to address their needs and support their sustainable development aspirations. This section explores the milestones in international recognition of SIDS challenges, key initiatives, and partnerships aimed at advancing sustainable development in these vulnerable regions.

United Nations Conference on the Human Environment (Stockholm, 1972):

The United Nations Conference on the Human Environment in Stockholm marked a turning point in global environmental awareness, raising concerns about the ecological impacts of development and pollution. SIDS representatives highlighted the disproportionate vulnerability of their countries to environmental degradation and the urgent need for international support.

United Nations Convention on the Law of the Sea (UNCLOS, 1982):

The adoption of the United Nations Convention on the Law of the Sea (UNCLOS) recognized SIDS' rights and interests in their maritime zones, including exclusive economic zones (EEZs) and extended continental shelves. UNCLOS provided a legal framework for the sustainable management of marine resources and the protection of marine ecosystems in SIDS.

Barbados Programme of Action (BPOA, 1994):

The Barbados Programme of Action (BPOA) emerged from the Global Conference on the Sustainable Development of SIDS, held in Barbados in 1994. BPOA identified the priority areas for action in SIDS, including climate change, natural disasters, sustainable tourism, biodiversity conservation, and sustainable energy, laying the foundation for international support and cooperation.

Mauritius Strategy for the Further Implementation of the BPOA (MSI, 2005):

The Mauritius Strategy for the Further Implementation of the BPOA (MSI) reaffirmed the commitments made under the BPOA and provided a roadmap for advancing sustainable development in SIDS. MSI emphasized the need for partnerships, capacity-building, and resource mobilization to address the challenges facing SIDS comprehensively.

United Nations Framework Convention on Climate Change (UNFCCC) and Kyoto Protocol:

SIDS have been vocal advocates for climate action within the United Nations Framework Convention on Climate Change (UNFCCC) and its Kyoto Protocol. SIDS' vulnerability to climate change impacts, including sea-level rise, coastal erosion, and extreme weather events, has underscored the urgency of global mitigation and adaptation efforts.

SIDS Accelerated Modalities of Action (SAMOA) Pathway (2014):

The SAMOA Pathway emerged from the Third International Conference on SIDS, held in Samoa in 2014, as a renewed commitment to supporting sustainable development in SIDS. SAMOA Pathway identified priority areas for action, including climate change, sustainable energy, oceans, biodiversity, and resilience-building, and called for enhanced international cooperation and partnerships.

Sustainable Development Goals (SDGs):

The Sustainable Development Goals (SDGs) recognize the unique development challenges faced by SIDS and provide a comprehensive framework for addressing them. SDG 14 (Life Below Water) and SDG 13 (Climate Action), in particular, focus on issues relevant to SIDS, such as ocean conservation, climate resilience, and sustainable energy.

Global Partnerships and Initiatives:

International organizations, donor agencies, development banks, and civil society groups have formed partnerships and initiatives to support sustainable development in SIDS. These include initiatives such as the Global Environment Facility (GEF) Small Grants Programme, the Alliance of Small Island States (AOSIS), and regional organizations like the Pacific Islands Forum (PIF) and the Caribbean Community (CARICOM).

In summary, the international recognition of Small Island Developing States' challenges has led to the development of targeted initiatives, partnerships, and commitments aimed at advancing their sustainable development goals. Despite progress, continued international cooperation and support are essential to address the complex and interconnected challenges facing SIDS and to ensure their resilience, prosperity, and well-being in the face of evolving global dynamics.

2.4 Milestones in Sustainable Development Efforts

Over the decades, SIDS have made significant strides in advancing sustainable development through various initiatives and partnerships:

- **Policy Frameworks:** Many SIDS have developed national sustainable development strategies and action plans to guide policy formulation and implementation. These frameworks integrate environmental protection, economic diversification, social inclusion, and cultural preservation, reflecting the holistic nature of sustainable development.

- **Regional Cooperation:** SIDS have strengthened regional cooperation and collaboration to address common challenges and leverage collective resources. Regional organizations such as the Pacific Islands Forum, Caribbean Community (CARICOM), and Indian Ocean Commission facilitate knowledge sharing, capacity building, and joint initiatives in areas such as climate change adaptation, disaster risk reduction, and sustainable tourism.

- **International Partnerships:** SIDS engage with international partners, including governments, multilateral organizations, civil society, and the private sector, to mobilize financial resources, technical expertise, and technology transfer for sustainable development projects. Initiatives such as the Alliance of Small Island States (AOSIS) and the Global Island Partnership (GLISPA) advocate for SIDS interests on the global stage and promote innovative solutions to common challenges.

A detail on each point is elaborated in the section that follows. Small Island Developing States (SIDS) have achieved significant milestones in their pursuit of sustainable development, overcoming challenges and leveraging opportunities to advance their socio-economic, environmental, and governance agendas. This section highlights key milestones in SIDS' sustainable development efforts, showcasing initiatives, policies, and achievements that have contributed to their resilience, prosperity, and well-being.

1. Establishment of Regional Organizations:

Regional organizations, such as the Pacific Islands Forum (PIF), the Caribbean Community (CARICOM), and the Indian Ocean Commission (IOC), have played a crucial role in fostering regional cooperation, integration, and solidarity among SIDS. These platforms provide opportunities for SIDS to address common challenges, share best practices, and advocate for their interests on the global stage.

2. Adoption of Sustainable Development Plans:

Many SIDS have developed national sustainable development plans, strategies, and frameworks to guide their development priorities and actions. These plans integrate environmental conservation, climate resilience, social inclusion, and economic diversification objectives, reflecting the holistic approach to sustainable development embraced by SIDS.

3. Renewable Energy Transitions:

SIDS have made significant strides in transitioning to renewable energy sources to reduce their dependency on imported fossil fuels, mitigate climate change impacts, and enhance energy security. Initiatives such as the Pacific Islands Renewable Energy Project (PIREP) and the Caribbean Sustainable Energy Roadmap and Strategy (C-SERMS) have facilitated investments in solar, wind, hydro, and geothermal energy projects.

4. Marine Conservation and Blue Economy Initiatives:

SIDS have prioritized marine conservation and sustainable ocean management as integral components of their sustainable development agendas. Marine protected areas (MPAs), coral reef restoration projects, and sustainable fisheries management initiatives have been established to conserve biodiversity, promote sustainable livelihoods, and harness the potential of the blue economy.

5. Climate Resilience and Adaptation Measures:

SIDS have implemented climate resilience and adaptation measures to address the impacts of climate change, including sea-level rise, coastal erosion, and extreme weather events. These measures encompass coastal protection, disaster risk reduction, ecosystem-based adaptation, and climate-resilient infrastructure projects aimed at enhancing community resilience and safeguarding livelihoods.

6. Community-Based Tourism and Sustainable Livelihoods:

Community-based tourism initiatives have empowered local communities in SIDS to participate in and benefit from the tourism industry while preserving their cultural heritage and natural resources. These initiatives promote sustainable tourism practices, eco-friendly accommodations, and cultural experiences, contributing to poverty alleviation and inclusive economic growth.

7. Sustainable Agriculture and Food Security Programs:

SIDS have implemented sustainable agriculture and food security programs to enhance food self-sufficiency, promote agroecological practices, and address nutrition challenges. Initiatives such as organic farming, agroforestry, and climate-smart agriculture projects support smallholder farmers, improve resilience to climate variability, and ensure food sovereignty in SIDS.

8. Access to Clean Water and Sanitation:

Efforts to improve access to clean water and sanitation have been prioritized in SIDS to address water scarcity, promote public health, and ensure environmental sustainability. Investments in water infrastructure, rainwater harvesting, water conservation measures, and wastewater treatment facilities have expanded access to safe drinking water and sanitation services in SIDS communities.

9. Strengthening Governance and Institutional Capacity:

SIDS have focused on strengthening governance systems and building institutional capacity to enhance policy coherence, transparency, and accountability in sustainable development decision-making. Initiatives such as capacity-building programs, institutional reforms, and anti-corruption measures have aimed to improve governance effectiveness and promote sustainable development outcomes.

In summary, Small Island Developing States (SIDS) have achieved significant milestones in their sustainable development journey, demonstrating resilience, innovation, and commitment to addressing the complex challenges they face. Through partnerships, investments, and policy reforms, SIDS continue to advance their sustainable development agendas, striving for inclusive, equitable, and resilient futures for their people and environments.

Chapter – 3

Environmental Conservation and Biodiversity in SIDS

The small size and unique ecosystems of Small Island Developing States (SIDS) render them particularly vulnerable to environmental degradation and loss of biodiversity. This chapter explores the fragile ecosystems of SIDS, the threats they face, conservation efforts, and the integration of traditional knowledge with modern conservation practices.

3.1 Fragile Ecosystems of SIDS

Small Island Developing States (SIDS) are endowed with diverse and fragile ecosystems that play a critical role in supporting livelihoods, biodiversity, and cultural heritage. This section delves into the unique ecosystems found in SIDS, their ecological significance, and the challenges they face due to human activities, climate change, and environmental degradation.

1. Coral Reefs:

Coral reefs are among the most biodiverse and economically valuable ecosystems in SIDS, providing habitats for marine species, coastal protection, and livelihood opportunities for local communities. These delicate ecosystems are threatened by climate change-induced coral bleaching, ocean acidification, overfishing, pollution, and destructive fishing practices, jeopardizing their ecological integrity and resilience.

2. Mangrove Forests:

Mangrove forests are vital coastal ecosystems found in many SIDS, serving as nurseries for fish and other marine species, carbon sinks, and buffers against storm surges and coastal erosion. Despite their ecological importance, mangrove forests are under threat from urbanization, aquaculture expansion, deforestation, and pollution, leading to habitat loss and degradation.

3. Tropical Rainforests:

Tropical rainforests are rich biodiversity hotspots found in SIDS such as Fiji, Papua New Guinea, and Dominica, harboring endemic species of plants, animals, and insects. These forests provide essential ecosystem services, including carbon sequestration, watershed protection, and soil fertility. However, deforestation, land conversion, and unsustainable logging practices pose significant threats to their conservation and long-term sustainability.

4. Coastal and Marine Ecosystems:

Coastal and marine ecosystems, including seagrass beds, lagoons, and estuaries, are integral to the ecological and socio-economic well-being of SIDS. These ecosystems support fisheries, tourism, recreation, and cultural practices, but are vulnerable to pollution, habitat destruction, and coastal development activities. Sustainable management and conservation efforts are essential to preserve their ecological functions and resilience.

5. Island Biodiversity:

SIDS are home to unique and endemic species of flora and fauna adapted to their island environments. Island biodiversity is characterized by high levels of endemism, genetic diversity, and species richness, making SIDS biodiversity hotspots of global significance. However, invasive species, habitat loss, climate change, and unsustainable land use practices threaten island biodiversity, necessitating conservation actions and protected area management.

6. Freshwater Ecosystems:

Freshwater ecosystems, including rivers, lakes, and wetlands, are essential sources of freshwater, biodiversity, and ecosystem services in SIDS. These ecosystems support agriculture, fisheries, and drinking water supply for local communities but are vulnerable to pollution, habitat degradation, and water scarcity. Sustainable water management practices are crucial to ensure the availability and quality of freshwater resources in SIDS.

7. High-Elevation Ecosystems:

High-elevation ecosystems, such as mountain forests and alpine grasslands, are found in SIDS with volcanic or mountainous terrain, such as Hawaii, Samoa, and St. Lucia. These ecosystems provide critical habitats for unique species, regulate water flow, and contribute to watershed protection. Climate change impacts, including temperature rise and invasive species encroachment, pose threats to the biodiversity and ecological balance of high-elevation ecosystems.

In summary, the fragile ecosystems of Small Island Developing States (SIDS) are under increasing pressure from human activities, climate change, and environmental degradation. Protecting and conserving these ecosystems are paramount for safeguarding biodiversity, supporting sustainable livelihoods, and ensuring the resilience and well-being of SIDS communities and environments.

3.2 Threats to Biodiversity

Biodiversity, the variety of life on Earth, is fundamental to the health and resilience of ecosystems and essential for sustaining life. However, Small Island Developing States (SIDS) face numerous threats to biodiversity, stemming from human activities, habitat loss, invasive species, climate change, and pollution. This section explores the major threats to biodiversity in SIDS and their implications for ecosystems, economies, and human well-being.

1. Habitat Loss and Fragmentation:

Habitat loss and fragmentation are among the leading threats to biodiversity in SIDS, driven by urbanization, agriculture expansion, infrastructure development, and land conversion for tourism and industrial activities. Deforestation, wetland drainage, and coastal development activities encroach upon natural habitats, fragmenting ecosystems and reducing the availability of suitable habitats for species.

2. Invasive Alien Species:

Invasive alien species pose significant threats to native biodiversity in SIDS, outcompeting native species for resources, altering ecosystem dynamics, and disrupting ecological processes. Invasive species, such as rats, feral cats, invasive plants, and introduced pathogens, can lead to the decline or extinction of native species, particularly endemic species found only in SIDS.

3. Overexploitation of Natural Resources:

Overexploitation of natural resources, including fisheries, forests, and wildlife, threatens biodiversity in SIDS, depleting populations of commercially valuable species and disrupting ecological balance. Unsustainable fishing practices, illegal logging, poaching, and wildlife trafficking contribute to species decline, ecosystem degradation, and loss of ecosystem services.

4. Climate Change Impacts:

Climate change poses significant threats to biodiversity in SIDS, altering habitats, disrupting species distributions, and increasing the frequency and intensity of extreme weather events. Rising temperatures, sea-level rise, ocean acidification, and changing precipitation patterns affect ecosystems such as coral reefs, mangroves, and high-elevation habitats, jeopardizing the survival of species adapted to specific environmental conditions.

5. Pollution and Contamination:

Pollution and contamination from industrial activities, agriculture runoff, waste disposal, and marine debris pose threats to biodiversity in SIDS, impacting terrestrial, freshwater, and marine ecosystems. Pollution reduces water quality, contaminates soil, and harms aquatic organisms, leading to biodiversity loss, ecosystem degradation, and public health risks in SIDS communities.

6. Unsustainable Land Use Practices:

Unsustainable land use practices, including slash-and-burn agriculture, land clearing, and monoculture plantations, degrade habitats, reduce ecosystem resilience, and contribute to biodiversity decline in SIDS. Conversion of natural ecosystems into agricultural, urban, and industrial landscapes fragments habitats, disrupts ecological connectivity, and diminishes the ability of ecosystems to support diverse species.

7. Coastal Development and Habitat Destruction:

Coastal development and habitat destruction pose significant threats to coastal and marine biodiversity in SIDS, altering coastal ecosystems, degrading coral reefs, and reducing nesting habitats for marine species. Infrastructure projects, coastal engineering works, and tourism developments exacerbate habitat loss, coastal erosion, and sedimentation, threatening the integrity and resilience of coastal ecosystems.

8. Population Growth and Urbanization:

Population growth and urbanization in SIDS increase pressure on natural resources, intensify land use conflicts, and contribute to habitat fragmentation and degradation. Urban expansion, informal settlements, and infrastructure development encroach upon natural habitats, exacerbating biodiversity loss and environmental degradation in peri-urban and coastal areas.

In summary, Small Island Developing States (SIDS) face multifaceted threats to biodiversity, stemming from habitat loss, invasive species, overexploitation of natural resources, climate change impacts, pollution, unsustainable land use practices, coastal development, and population growth. Addressing these threats requires integrated approaches, policy interventions, and community engagement to conserve and sustainably manage biodiversity for the benefit of present and future generations.

3.3 Conservation Efforts and Success Stories

In the face of mounting threats to biodiversity, Small Island Developing States (SIDS) have implemented a variety of conservation efforts and initiatives to protect and preserve their unique ecosystems and species. This section explores some of the conservation efforts undertaken in SIDS, highlighting success stories and innovative approaches that have contributed to biodiversity conservation and sustainable resource management.

1. Establishment of Protected Areas:

SIDS have designated and managed protected areas to conserve biodiversity, preserve ecosystems, and safeguard critical habitats. These protected areas, including national parks, marine reserves, and wildlife sanctuaries, serve as refuges for threatened species, promote ecosystem resilience, and support sustainable tourism and recreation. Success stories include the Seychelles' Aldabra Atoll UNESCO World Heritage Site and Palau's Protected Areas Network.

2. Community-Based Conservation Initiatives:

Community-based conservation initiatives empower local communities in SIDS to participate in and benefit from biodiversity conservation efforts. These initiatives engage communities in conservation planning, natural resource management, and sustainable livelihoods, fostering stewardship and ownership of natural resources. Success stories include Fiji's Locally Managed Marine Areas (LMMA) network and the Community Conservation Areas in Papua New Guinea.

3. Invasive Species Management Programs:

SIDS have implemented invasive species management programs to control and eradicate invasive alien species threatening native biodiversity. These programs employ techniques such as biosecurity measures, eradication campaigns, and habitat restoration to prevent the spread of invasive species and restore native ecosystems. Success stories include the eradication of invasive rats from Henderson Island in the Pitcairn Islands and efforts to control invasive lionfish in the Caribbean.

4. Sustainable Fisheries Management:

Sustainable fisheries management is crucial for preserving marine biodiversity and ensuring the long-term viability of fish stocks in SIDS. SIDS have implemented measures such as fisheries regulations, marine protected areas, and community-based fisheries management to promote sustainable fishing practices, reduce overfishing, and conserve marine ecosystems. Success stories include the implementation of community-based fisheries management in the Solomon Islands and the establishment of no-take zones in Seychelles.

5. Conservation Partnerships and Collaborations:

SIDS have forged partnerships and collaborations with international organizations, donor agencies, and civil society groups to strengthen biodiversity conservation efforts. These partnerships provide technical expertise, financial support, and capacity-building opportunities to enhance conservation initiatives and promote knowledge sharing. Success stories include the Pacific Islands Biodiversity Partnership (PIBP) and the Caribbean Challenge Initiative (CCI).

6. Climate Resilience and Adaptation Measures:

Climate resilience and adaptation measures play a crucial role in safeguarding biodiversity and ecosystem services in SIDS. SIDS have implemented ecosystem-based adaptation strategies, coastal protection measures, and climate-smart agriculture practices to enhance ecosystem resilience and support species adaptation to changing environmental conditions. Success stories include the restoration of mangrove ecosystems in Grenada and the implementation of climate-resilient agricultural practices in Samoa.

In summary, Small Island Developing States (SIDS) have demonstrated their commitment to biodiversity conservation through a variety of innovative initiatives and partnerships. Despite the challenges they face, SIDS continue to make significant strides in protecting their unique ecosystems and species, ensuring a sustainable future for both nature and people.

3.4 Integrating Traditional Knowledge with Modern Conservation Practices

SIDS recognize the value of traditional knowledge systems in conserving biodiversity and managing natural resources sustainably. Indigenous and local communities possess traditional ecological knowledge (TEK) accumulated over generations, which complements scientific expertise and informs conservation practices. By integrating traditional knowledge with modern conservation approaches, SIDS can enhance the effectiveness and cultural relevance of conservation efforts. Strategies for integrating traditional knowledge include:

- **Collaborative Resource Management:** Engaging indigenous and local communities in decision-making processes and co-management of protected areas fosters mutual respect, enhances community ownership, and promotes stewardship of natural resources.

- **Indigenous Practices and Technologies:** Incorporating traditional ecological practices, such as agroforestry, traditional fisheries management, and traditional seed saving techniques, into conservation strategies can enhance ecosystem resilience and promote sustainable livelihoods.

- **Knowledge Exchange and Capacity Building:** Facilitating knowledge exchange between traditional knowledge holders, scientists, and policymakers fosters mutual learning, builds trust, and strengthens local capacity for biodiversity conservation.

- **Cultural Revitalization:** Recognizing and celebrating indigenous cultures, languages, and traditions fosters pride and resilience among indigenous communities, reinforcing their connection to the land and motivating them to conserve biodiversity.

By harnessing the synergies between traditional knowledge and modern conservation practices, SIDS can enhance the sustainability of their conservation efforts and safeguard their unique biodiversity for future generations.

In Small Island Developing States (SIDS), traditional knowledge systems have long provided valuable insights into sustainable resource management, biodiversity conservation, and ecosystem resilience. Integrating traditional knowledge with modern conservation practices offers a holistic approach to biodiversity conservation and promotes culturally appropriate solutions to environmental challenges. This section explores the importance of integrating traditional knowledge with modern conservation practices in SIDS and showcases examples of successful integration efforts.

1. Recognizing the Value of Traditional Knowledge:

Traditional knowledge, passed down through generations by indigenous peoples and local communities in SIDS, encompasses a deep understanding of ecosystems, species interactions, and natural resource management practices. This knowledge is often based on centuries of observation, experimentation, and adaptation to local environmental conditions, offering unique insights into sustainable living and coexistence with nature.

2. Complementarity of Traditional and Scientific Knowledge:

Traditional knowledge complements scientific knowledge by providing context-specific information, practical solutions, and holistic perspectives on environmental issues. Indigenous knowledge systems often incorporate sophisticated ecological knowledge, traditional land-use practices, and cultural values that inform sustainable resource management strategies and conservation practices.

3. Sustainable Resource Management Practices:

Traditional resource management practices in SIDS, such as rotational farming, agroforestry, community-based fisheries management, and sacred groves, promote biodiversity conservation, soil fertility, and ecosystem resilience. Integrating these traditional practices with modern conservation approaches enhances the effectiveness and sustainability of conservation efforts, while respecting cultural heritage and indigenous rights.

4. Indigenous Governance and Stewardship:

Indigenous governance systems in SIDS, including customary laws, traditional leadership structures, and communal decision-making processes, play a crucial role in conserving biodiversity and managing natural resources. Recognizing and supporting indigenous governance and stewardship initiatives strengthens local ownership, fosters community participation, and enhances the resilience of ecosystems.

5. Climate Change Adaptation and Resilience:

Traditional knowledge offers valuable insights into climate change adaptation and resilience-building strategies in SIDS. Indigenous peoples and local communities have developed adaptive strategies, such as diversified cropping systems, traditional water harvesting techniques, and knowledge of seasonal weather patterns, to cope with climate variability and extreme events.

6. Reviving Traditional Practices and Revitalizing Indigenous Knowledge:

Efforts to revive traditional practices and revitalize indigenous knowledge systems in SIDS contribute to cultural continuity, community empowerment, and sustainable development. Initiatives such as cultural heritage preservation, indigenous language revitalization, and intergenerational knowledge exchange strengthen the resilience of indigenous communities and promote cultural diversity and identity.

7. Participatory Conservation and Co-Management Approaches:

Incorporating traditional knowledge holders and local communities into conservation decision-making processes fosters inclusive and participatory approaches to biodiversity conservation in SIDS. Co-management arrangements, where indigenous peoples and local communities collaborate with government agencies and conservation organizations, promote shared stewardship, mutual respect, and equitable benefit-sharing.

8. Policy Support and Institutional Recognition:

Policy support and institutional recognition of traditional knowledge systems are essential for mainstreaming indigenous perspectives into conservation policies, programs, and strategies. SIDS governments and international organizations are increasingly recognizing the importance of traditional knowledge in biodiversity conservation and adopting policies that promote its integration into conservation practices.

In summary, integrating traditional knowledge with modern conservation practices offers a holistic and culturally sensitive approach to biodiversity conservation in Small Island Developing States (SIDS). By harnessing the wisdom of indigenous peoples and local communities, SIDS can enhance the effectiveness, equity, and sustainability of conservation efforts, ensuring the preservation of biodiversity and cultural heritage for future generations.

Chapter – 4

- Economic Decline
- Loss of Marine and coastal biodiversity
- Sea-level Rise (SLR)
- Loss of heritage and cultural resources
- **Vulnerabilities of the SIDS**
- Loss of Terrestrial biodiversity/ecosystems
- Health and Well-being
- Loss and Damage of settlements and infrastructure
- Water Security

Climate Change and Resilience Building in SIDS

Small Island Developing States (SIDS) face disproportionate challenges in combating climate change due to their geographic location, limited resources, and high vulnerability to its impacts. This chapter examines the unique vulnerabilities of SIDS to climate change, explores adaptation and mitigation strategies, and highlights international collaboration efforts aimed at building resilience.

4.1 Vulnerability to Climate Change

Small Island Developing States (SIDS) are among the most vulnerable regions to the impacts of climate change due to their geographical, socio-economic, and environmental characteristics. This section explores the unique vulnerabilities of SIDS to climate change and the implications for ecosystems, economies, and communities.

1. Geographic Exposure:

SIDS are situated in low-lying coastal areas, making them highly susceptible to sea-level rise, storm surges, and coastal erosion. Many SIDS have small landmasses, limited elevation, and dense populations concentrated along coastal areas, exacerbating their exposure to climate-related hazards and increasing the risk of displacement, infrastructure damage, and loss of livelihoods.

2. Climate-Sensitive Economies:

SIDS economies are heavily reliant on climate-sensitive sectors such as tourism, agriculture, fisheries, and coastal industries. Climate change impacts, including coral bleaching, ocean acidification, extreme weather events, and sea-level rise, threaten the viability of these sectors, disrupting supply chains, reducing productivity, and undermining economic stability in SIDS.

3. Fragile Ecosystems and Biodiversity Loss:

SIDS' fragile ecosystems, including coral reefs, mangroves, and tropical rainforests, are highly vulnerable to climate change impacts, such as temperature rise, ocean acidification, and extreme weather events. Biodiversity loss, habitat degradation, and ecosystem disruptions threaten the resilience of

SIDS ecosystems, jeopardizing ecosystem services, food security, and cultural heritage.

4. Water Scarcity and Coastal Salinization:

Climate change exacerbates water scarcity and coastal salinization in SIDS, affecting freshwater resources, agricultural productivity, and public health. Rising temperatures, changing precipitation patterns, and sea-level rise alter hydrological cycles, reducing water availability and increasing the intrusion of saltwater into coastal aquifers, threatening drinking water supplies and agricultural lands.

5. Food Insecurity and Nutrition Challenges:

Climate change impacts, such as changing rainfall patterns, increased temperatures, and extreme weather events, exacerbate food insecurity and nutrition challenges in SIDS. Disruptions to agricultural production, fisheries, and food supply chains compromise food access, affordability, and dietary diversity, exacerbating malnutrition and health risks in vulnerable populations.

6. Health Risks and Vector-Borne Diseases:

Climate change increases the prevalence of vector-borne diseases, such as dengue fever, malaria, and Zika virus, in SIDS, posing significant health risks to populations. Warmer temperatures, changing precipitation patterns, and habitat disruptions create favorable conditions for disease vectors to proliferate, leading to increased disease transmission and public health impacts.

7. Loss of Cultural Heritage and Identity:

Climate change threatens the loss of cultural heritage and traditional knowledge in SIDS, undermining indigenous cultures, languages, and practices. Rising sea levels, coastal erosion, and extreme weather events endanger cultural sites, sacred places, and cultural practices, eroding the identity and resilience of indigenous peoples and local communities.

8. Limited Adaptive Capacity and Financial Constraints:

SIDS face challenges in building adaptive capacity and resilience to climate change due to limited financial resources, institutional capacity constraints, and dependency on external assistance. The high cost of climate adaptation measures, inadequate infrastructure, and competing development priorities hamper efforts to mainstream climate resilience into national policies and strategies.

In summary, Small Island Developing States (SIDS) are highly vulnerable to the impacts of climate change, posing significant challenges to their ecosystems, economies, and communities. Addressing climate change requires coordinated action, adaptation strategies, and international cooperation to build resilience, reduce vulnerabilities, and ensure sustainable development in SIDS.

4.2 Adaptation Strategies

To cope with the adverse impacts of climate change, SIDS have been implementing adaptation strategies tailored to their unique circumstances:

- **Coastal Protection Measures:** SIDS invest in coastal protection infrastructure such as seawalls, dikes, and beach nourishment to reduce erosion, flooding, and saltwater intrusion.

- **Climate-Resilient Infrastructure:** SIDS integrate climate resilience considerations into infrastructure planning and design, incorporating features such as elevated buildings, storm water management systems, and green infrastructure.

- **Diversification of Livelihoods:** SIDS promote economic diversification to reduce dependence on climate-sensitive sectors, encouraging entrepreneurship, skills development, and alternative livelihood options.

- **Ecosystem-Based Adaptation:** SIDS employ ecosystem-based approaches to adaptation, such as mangrove restoration, coral reef protection, and sustainable land management, to enhance ecosystem resilience and provide natural buffers against climate impacts.

- **Early Warning Systems:** SIDS establish and strengthen early warning systems to alert communities to impending natural hazards, enabling timely evacuation and emergency response.

These adaptation measures aim to enhance SIDS' resilience to climate change impacts and build adaptive capacity at the national and community levels and each one is detailed hereinafter.

In response to the existential threat posed by climate change, Small Island Developing States (SIDS) have been proactive in implementing adaptation strategies to build resilience, reduce vulnerability, and safeguard their socio-economic and environmental systems. This section explores the adaptation strategies employed by SIDS to address the diverse and multifaceted challenges posed by climate change.

1. Coastal Protection and Infrastructure Resilience:

SIDS are implementing coastal protection measures, including the construction of seawalls, breakwaters, and artificial reefs, to mitigate the impacts of sea-level rise, storm surges, and coastal erosion. Enhancing the resilience of coastal infrastructure, such as roads, buildings, and water supply systems, reduces the risk of damage and disruption from extreme weather events and rising sea levels.

2. Climate-Resilient Agriculture and Food Security:

SIDS are adopting climate-resilient agricultural practices, such as crop diversification, soil conservation, agroforestry, and water-efficient irrigation techniques, to enhance food security and adapt to changing climatic conditions. Sustainable agriculture initiatives promote resilient crop varieties, drought-tolerant crops, and climate-smart farming practices that improve productivity and mitigate climate risks.

3. Sustainable Water Management and Conservation:

SIDS are implementing sustainable water management strategies to address water scarcity, ensure reliable access to clean water, and reduce the risk of droughts and water-related disasters. Rainwater harvesting, water recycling, groundwater recharge, and desalination technologies help conserve freshwater resources, enhance water security, and support sustainable development in SIDS.

4. Ecosystem-Based Adaptation and Biodiversity Conservation:

SIDS are prioritizing ecosystem-based adaptation approaches that harness the natural resilience of ecosystems to enhance climate resilience and biodiversity conservation. Protecting and restoring coastal habitats, such as mangroves, coral reefs, and sea grass beds, provides natural buffers against storm surges, supports fisheries, and sequesters carbon, contributing to climate mitigation and adaptation goals.

5. Disaster Risk Reduction and Early Warning Systems:

SIDS are strengthening disaster risk reduction measures and early warning systems to enhance preparedness, response, and recovery from climate-related disasters. Investing in disaster-resilient infrastructure, emergency shelters, and community-based early warning systems helps mitigate the impacts of hurricanes, cyclones, floods, and other extreme events on vulnerable populations.

6. Renewable Energy Transition and Energy Security:

SIDS are transitioning to renewable energy sources, such as solar, wind, hydro, and geothermal energy, to reduce reliance on imported fossil fuels, mitigate greenhouse gas emissions, and enhance energy security. Renewable energy projects, energy efficiency measures, and decentralized energy systems help diversify energy sources, improve access to clean energy, and promote sustainable development in SIDS.

7. Community-Based Adaptation and Local Resilience:

SIDS are fostering community-based adaptation initiatives that empower local communities to identify and address climate risks, build resilience, and adapt to changing environmental conditions. Community-led initiatives, such as mangrove restoration, rainwater harvesting, and climate-resilient livelihoods, promote social cohesion, knowledge exchange, and adaptive capacity at the grassroots level.

8. Mainstreaming Climate Resilience into Policies and Planning:

SIDS are mainstreaming climate resilience into national policies, plans, and strategies to integrate climate considerations into development decision-making processes. Climate-proofing infrastructure, land-use planning, and development projects, and incorporating climate risk assessments into sectoral policies help mainstream climate resilience and ensure sustainable development pathways in SIDS.

In summary, Small Island Developing States (SIDS) are implementing a diverse range of adaptation strategies to address the complex and interconnected challenges posed by climate change. By building resilience, enhancing adaptive capacity, and mainstreaming climate considerations into development planning, SIDS are striving to secure a sustainable and climate-resilient future for their people and environments.

4.3 Mitigation Efforts

While Small Island Developing States (SIDS) are disproportionately affected by climate change, they are also committed to mitigating its impacts through various efforts aimed at reducing greenhouse gas emissions and promoting sustainable development. This section explores the mitigation efforts undertaken by SIDS to combat climate change and contribute to global efforts to limit temperature rise.

1. Renewable Energy Transition:

SIDS are investing in renewable energy sources, such as solar, wind, hydro, and geothermal energy, to reduce reliance on imported fossil fuels and mitigate greenhouse gas emissions. Renewable energy projects, including solar photovoltaic installations, wind farms, and mini-hydro plants, enhance energy security, promote local employment, and contribute to decarbonizing the energy sector in SIDS.

2. Energy Efficiency Measures:

SIDS are implementing energy efficiency measures to reduce energy consumption, improve energy efficiency, and lower greenhouse gas emissions across various sectors, including transportation, buildings, and industry. Initiatives such as energy-efficient lighting, appliance standards, building codes, and public transportation systems help reduce carbon footprints and enhance sustainability in SIDS.

3. Reforestation and Afforestation Programs:

SIDS are undertaking reforestation and afforestation programs to enhance carbon sequestration, restore degraded ecosystems, and mitigate deforestation-driven emissions. Planting native tree species, restoring mangrove forests, and implementing agroforestry initiatives sequester carbon dioxide from the atmosphere, promote biodiversity conservation, and enhance ecosystem resilience in SIDS.

4. Sustainable Land Use and Agriculture Practices:

SIDS are promoting sustainable land use and agriculture practices that reduce emissions from deforestation, land degradation, and agricultural activities. Agroecological practices, such as organic farming, agroforestry, and conservation agriculture, enhance soil carbon sequestration, improve resilience to climate change, and promote food security and livelihoods in SIDS.

5. Blue Carbon Initiatives:

SIDS are harnessing the carbon sequestration potential of coastal and marine ecosystems, known as blue carbon, to mitigate climate change impacts. Protecting and restoring mangrove forests, seagrass meadows, and salt marshes sequesters carbon dioxide from the atmosphere, enhances coastal resilience, and conserves biodiversity in SIDS coastal areas.

6. Waste Management and Circular Economy:

SIDS are implementing waste management strategies and transitioning towards circular economy models to reduce greenhouse gas emissions from waste generation and disposal. Recycling programs, waste-to-energy facilities, and composting initiatives help minimize methane emissions from landfills, promote resource efficiency, and contribute to climate mitigation efforts in SIDS.

7. Low-Carbon Transport Solutions:

SIDS are promoting low-carbon transport solutions, including public transportation systems, electric vehicles, and non-motorized transport options, to reduce emissions from the transportation sector. Investing in clean and efficient transport infrastructure, promoting cycling and walking, and adopting fuel-efficient vehicles help mitigate air pollution, congestion, and greenhouse gas emissions in SIDS.

8. International Cooperation and Climate Finance:

SIDS are advocating for international cooperation and climate finance support to enhance their mitigation efforts and transition to low-carbon, climate-resilient economies. Accessing climate finance mechanisms, such as the Green Climate Fund (GCF) and Global Environment Facility (GEF), enables SIDS to implement mitigation projects, build institutional capacity, and accelerate the transition to a sustainable future.

In summary, Small Island Developing States (SIDS) are implementing a range of mitigation efforts to reduce greenhouse gas emissions, enhance carbon sequestration, and promote sustainable development pathways. By adopting renewable energy, enhancing energy efficiency, promoting sustainable land use practices, and accessing climate finance, SIDS are demonstrating their commitment to combating climate change and contributing to global climate action.

4.4 International Collaboration on Climate Change Resilience

Recognizing the shared vulnerabilities and challenges posed by climate change, Small Island Developing States (SIDS) have been actively engaged in international collaboration efforts to strengthen climate resilience, build adaptive capacity, and mobilize support for climate action. This section explores the importance of international collaboration in addressing climate change resilience in SIDS and showcases examples of successful partnerships and initiatives.

1. United Nations Framework Convention on Climate Change (UNFCCC):

SIDS actively participate in the United Nations Framework Convention on Climate Change (UNFCCC) negotiations, advocating for ambitious emission reduction targets, adaptation support, and climate finance for vulnerable countries. Through the Conference of the Parties (COP) meetings, SIDS amplify their voices, raise awareness of their unique vulnerabilities, and push for global action on climate change.

2. Paris Agreement Implementation:

SIDS played a crucial role in shaping the Paris Agreement, a landmark international treaty aimed at limiting global temperature rise to well below 2 degrees Celsius above pre-industrial levels. SIDS are committed to implementing their Nationally Determined Contributions (NDCs) under the Paris Agreement, which outline their mitigation and adaptation actions to address climate change impacts.

3. Climate Finance and Support Mechanisms:

SIDS rely on climate finance and support mechanisms to finance their adaptation and mitigation efforts, build resilience, and address loss and damage associated with climate change impacts. Accessing climate finance sources, such as the Green Climate Fund (GCF), Adaptation Fund, and Global Environment Facility (GEF), enables SIDS to implement priority projects and programs that enhance climate resilience and sustainability.

4. Regional Collaboration and Partnerships:

SIDS engage in regional collaboration and partnerships to address shared climate change challenges, exchange knowledge and best practices, and leverage collective resources for adaptation and mitigation initiatives. Regional organizations, such as the Caribbean Community (CARICOM), Pacific Islands Forum (PIF), and Indian Ocean Commission (IOC), facilitate coordination, capacity-building, and joint action on climate resilience in SIDS regions.

5. South-South Cooperation and Knowledge Exchange:

SIDS participate in South-South cooperation initiatives and knowledge exchange platforms to share experiences, lessons learned, and innovative solutions for climate resilience. Peer-to-peer learning networks, twinning arrangements, and technical assistance programs facilitate collaboration among SIDS, enabling them to adapt and respond effectively to climate change impacts.

6. Technology Transfer and Innovation:

SIDS collaborate with developed countries, international organizations, and private sector partners to facilitate technology transfer, innovation, and capacity-building for climate resilience. Access to climate-resilient technologies, such as renewable energy systems, climate-smart agriculture practices, and disaster risk reduction tools, strengthens SIDS' adaptive capacity and promotes sustainable development pathways.

7. Capacity-Building and Institutional Support:

SIDS receive capacity-building and institutional support from international partners to strengthen their adaptive capacity, mainstream climate resilience into policies and planning, and enhance climate governance frameworks. Training programs, workshops, and technical assistance initiatives build local expertise, enhance institutional resilience, and empower SIDS to address climate change challenges effectively.

8. Advocacy and Leadership on Global Platforms:

SIDS advocate for their climate change resilience priorities and concerns on global platforms, such as the United Nations General Assembly, International Climate Summits, and High-Level Dialogues on Climate Change. By showcasing their experiences, highlighting their vulnerabilities, and calling for urgent action, SIDS mobilize international support and solidarity for climate resilience efforts.

Hence, it can be seen that, international collaboration plays a pivotal role in strengthening climate resilience and supporting sustainable development in Small Island Developing States (SIDS). By forging partnerships, accessing climate finance, sharing knowledge and technology, and advocating for their priorities on the global stage, SIDS amplify their resilience efforts and contribute to collective action on climate change mitigation and adaptation.

In summary, SIDS face significant challenges from climate change but are actively implementing adaptation and mitigation strategies while engaging in international collaboration to build resilience, reduce vulnerability, and secure a sustainable future for their citizens and ecosystems.

Chapter – 5

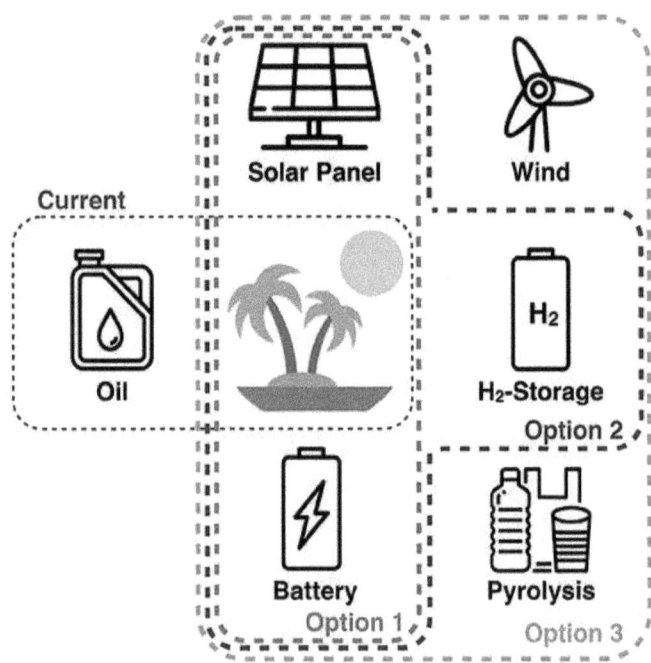

Sustainable Energy and Renewable Resources

Small Island Developing States (SIDS) encounter unique energy challenges due to their remote locations, limited access to traditional fuel sources, and vulnerability to external shocks. This chapter examines the energy landscape in SIDS, explores the transition to renewable energy sources, discusses innovative solutions in energy production and distribution, and evaluates policy frameworks for sustainable energy development.

5.1 Energy Challenges in SIDS

Small Island Developing States (SIDS) face unique energy challenges due to their small geographic size, limited resource endowment, vulnerability to external shocks, and high dependence on imported fossil fuels. This section examines the energy challenges encountered by SIDS and their implications for sustainable development, climate resilience, and energy security.

1. High Dependency on Imported Fossil Fuels:

SIDS rely heavily on imported fossil fuels, such as oil and diesel, for electricity generation, transportation, and industrial activities. The dependence on imported fuels exposes SIDS to volatile international oil prices, supply disruptions, and economic vulnerabilities, posing significant challenges to energy security and sustainability.

2. Cost and Affordability of Energy:

The high cost of imported fossil fuels in SIDS contributes to elevated energy prices, making electricity and fuel expenses disproportionately burdensome for households, businesses, and public institutions. Energy affordability challenges exacerbate poverty, hinder economic growth, and limit access to modern energy services, particularly for low-income communities in SIDS.

3. Climate Change Impacts on Energy Infrastructure:

SIDS' energy infrastructure is vulnerable to climate change impacts, including sea-level rise, extreme weather events, and coastal erosion. Coastal power plants, transmission lines, and fuel storage facilities are at risk of damage or disruption from storm surges, flooding, and saltwater intrusion, compromising energy reliability and resilience in SIDS.

4. Limited Access to Modern Energy Services:

Despite progress in electrification efforts, many remote and rural areas in SIDS still lack access to reliable and affordable electricity services. Inadequate energy infrastructure, geographical isolation, and financial constraints impede efforts to expand energy access, leaving marginalized communities underserved and reliant on traditional biomass for cooking and lighting.

5. Environmental and Health Impacts of Fossil Fuel Use:

The combustion of fossil fuels for energy production in SIDS contributes to air pollution, greenhouse gas emissions, and adverse health impacts on local populations. Emissions from power plants, vehicles, and industrial facilities degrade air quality, exacerbate respiratory illnesses, and contribute to climate change, posing risks to public health and environmental sustainability in SIDS.

6. Limited Renewable Energy Resources:

While SIDS possess abundant renewable energy resources, such as solar, wind, hydro, and geothermal energy, harnessing these resources faces technical, economic, and institutional challenges. Variable renewable energy availability, intermittent power generation, and grid integration constraints hinder the deployment of renewable energy technologies and the transition to a low-carbon energy future in SIDS.

7. Energy Inefficiency and Wastage:

SIDS often exhibit high levels of energy inefficiency and wastage due to outdated infrastructure, inefficient appliances, and inadequate energy conservation measures. Inefficient energy use increases energy consumption, greenhouse gas emissions, and energy costs, undermining efforts to achieve energy sustainability and climate resilience goals in SIDS.

8. Limited Institutional Capacity and Policy Frameworks:

SIDS face constraints in institutional capacity and policy frameworks for energy planning, regulation, and governance. Weak energy governance structures, inadequate technical expertise, and fragmented policy frameworks hamper efforts to formulate and implement effective energy policies, strategies, and regulations in SIDS.

In summary, Small Island Developing States (SIDS) encounter numerous energy challenges that hinder their efforts towards sustainable development, climate resilience, and energy security. Addressing these challenges requires integrated approaches, investment in renewable energy technologies, strengthening of energy governance frameworks, and international cooperation to support the transition to a sustainable and resilient energy future in SIDS.

5.2 Transitioning to Renewable Energy

To reduce dependency on imported fossil fuels and promote energy security, SIDS are increasingly embracing renewable energy sources:

- **Solar Power**: SIDS harness abundant solar resources through photovoltaic (PV) systems for electricity generation, solar water heaters for domestic hot water, and solar cookers for cooking.

- **Wind Energy:** SIDS leverage wind energy resources to install wind turbines for electricity generation, particularly in coastal and high-wind areas.

- **Hydropower:** SIDS tap into their hydrological resources to develop small-scale hydropower projects, providing clean and reliable electricity to remote communities.

- **Biomass and Bioenergy:** SIDS utilize locally available biomass resources, such as agricultural residues, organic waste, and forest biomass, to produce biofuels, biogas, and biomass-based electricity.
- **Ocean Energy:** SIDS explore ocean energy technologies, including wave energy, tidal energy, and ocean thermal energy conversion (OTEC), to harness the immense energy potential of the oceans.

Renewable energy deployment in SIDS offers multiple benefits, including reduced greenhouse gas emissions, improved energy access, enhanced energy resilience, and potential economic opportunities in the renewable energy sector.

In response to the energy challenges faced by Small Island Developing States (SIDS), there has been a growing recognition of the need to transition towards renewable energy sources. This section explores the transition to renewable energy in SIDS, examining the opportunities, challenges, and initiatives driving this shift towards a sustainable and resilient energy future.

1. Abundance of Renewable Energy Resources:

SIDS are endowed with abundant renewable energy resources, including solar, wind, hydro, geothermal, and biomass energy. Harnessing these indigenous resources offers SIDS the opportunity to reduce dependency on imported fossil fuels, enhance energy security, and mitigate greenhouse gas emissions, while promoting local economic development and resilience.

2. Solar Energy Deployment:

Solar energy holds immense potential for SIDS, given their year-round sunshine and tropical climate. SIDS are investing in solar photovoltaic (PV) systems for decentralized electricity generation, solar water heating for residential and commercial applications, and utility-scale solar projects to diversify their energy mix, reduce electricity costs, and expand energy access to remote areas.

3. Wind Energy Projects:

SIDS with suitable wind resources are exploring wind energy projects as a viable option for clean and renewable electricity generation. Wind farms, offshore wind turbines, and hybrid wind-diesel systems are being deployed in SIDS to harness wind power, stabilize electricity grids, and reduce reliance on imported diesel for power generation, contributing to climate mitigation efforts.

4. Hydropower Development:

SIDS with hydroelectric potential are developing small-scale hydropower projects to harness the energy of flowing water for electricity generation. Micro-hydro systems, run-of-river hydropower plants, and pumped storage facilities provide renewable energy solutions that are environmentally sustainable, socially inclusive, and economically viable for SIDS communities.

5. Geothermal Energy Utilization:

SIDS situated in geologically active regions have the opportunity to tap into geothermal energy resources for power generation, heating, and cooling applications. Geothermal power plants, direct-use systems, and geothermal heat pumps offer reliable and cost-effective renewable energy solutions that reduce greenhouse gas emissions and promote energy independence in SIDS.

6. Biomass and Bioenergy Initiatives:

SIDS are exploring biomass and bioenergy initiatives as alternative sources of renewable energy and sustainable fuels. Biomass gasification, biofuel production, and biogas digesters utilize organic waste, agricultural residues, and forest biomass to generate heat, electricity, and transportation fuels, reducing reliance on fossil fuels and promoting circular economy principles in SIDS.

7. Renewable Energy Integration and Grid Resilience:

Integrating renewable energy into existing electricity grids poses technical, regulatory, and institutional challenges for SIDS. Grid modernization, energy storage technologies, demand-side management, and smart grid solutions are being implemented to enhance grid flexibility, stability, and resilience, enabling greater penetration of intermittent renewable energy sources in SIDS power systems.

8. Policy Support and Investment Promotion:

SIDS governments are providing policy support and investment incentives to accelerate the transition to renewable energy. Renewable energy targets, feed-in tariffs, tax incentives, and regulatory frameworks facilitate private sector investment in renewable energy projects, stimulate innovation, and create opportunities for local entrepreneurship and job creation in SIDS.

In summary, transitioning to renewable energy offers Small Island Developing States (SIDS) a pathway towards sustainable development, climate resilience, and energy security. By harnessing their abundant renewable energy resources, SIDS can reduce dependency on imported fossil fuels, mitigate climate change impacts, and build resilient and inclusive energy systems that support economic growth and environmental sustainability.

5.3 Innovative Solutions in Energy Production and Distribution

Innovative solutions play a crucial role in overcoming technical, economic, and institutional barriers to sustainable energy deployment in SIDS:

- **Microgrid Systems:** SIDS deploy microgrid systems that integrate renewable energy sources, energy storage technologies, and smart grid components to provide reliable and resilient electricity supply to isolated communities.

- **Energy Storage Technologies:** SIDS invest in energy storage technologies, such as battery storage systems, pumped hydro storage, and thermal energy storage, to overcome intermittency challenges associated with renewable energy sources and enhance grid stability.

- **Off-Grid Solutions:** SIDS implement off-grid solutions, such as solar home systems, solar-powered water pumps, and standalone mini-grids, to extend electricity access to remote and underserved areas where grid extension is not feasible.

- **Energy Efficiency Measures:** SIDS prioritize energy efficiency measures, including energy-efficient appliances, building codes, lighting systems, and industrial processes, to reduce energy consumption, lower energy costs, and minimize environmental impacts.

These innovative solutions enable SIDS to overcome energy challenges, enhance energy resilience, and accelerate the transition to a sustainable energy future.

Small Island Developing States (SIDS) are at the forefront of adopting innovative solutions to overcome the unique energy challenges they face. This section delves into the innovative approaches SIDS are employing in energy production and distribution, highlighting technologies and strategies that enhance efficiency, reliability, and sustainability in their energy systems.

1. Microgrid Systems:

Microgrid systems offer decentralized energy solutions that provide reliable electricity access to remote and off-grid communities in SIDS. Incorporating renewable energy sources, energy storage systems, and smart grid technologies, microgrids improve energy reliability, resilience, and affordability, while reducing dependency on centralized power infrastructure and imported fossil fuels.

2. Energy Storage Technologies:

Energy storage technologies, such as batteries, pumped hydro storage, and thermal storage systems, play a critical role in balancing supply and demand, optimizing renewable energy integration, and enhancing grid stability in SIDS. Deploying energy storage solutions enables SIDS to store excess renewable energy during periods of low demand and utilize it during peak hours, reducing reliance on diesel generators and stabilizing electricity grids.

3. Smart Grid Solutions:

Smart grid solutions leverage advanced communication, automation, and control technologies to optimize energy production, distribution, and consumption in SIDS. Smart meters, grid sensors, and demand response systems enable real-time monitoring and management of electricity networks, improving grid efficiency, reducing losses, and enhancing energy resilience in SIDS.

4. Offshore Renewable Energy Projects:

SIDS are exploring offshore renewable energy projects, such as offshore wind farms, floating solar arrays, and marine energy systems, to harness untapped renewable energy resources and expand their clean energy capacity. Offshore renewable energy projects offer opportunities for large-scale electricity generation, job creation, and economic development while minimizing land use conflicts and environmental impacts in densely populated SIDS.

5. Hybrid Energy Systems:

Hybrid energy systems combine multiple renewable energy sources, such as solar, wind, hydro, and biomass, with energy storage technologies and backup generators to create resilient and cost-effective energy solutions in SIDS. Hybrid systems optimize resource utilization, mitigate intermittency challenges, and provide reliable electricity supply to remote and island communities, fostering energy independence and sustainability.

6. Peer-to-Peer Energy Trading Platforms:

Peer-to-peer energy trading platforms empower consumers in SIDS to buy, sell, and exchange excess renewable energy directly with neighboring households or businesses, bypassing traditional utility intermediaries. Blockchain technology, smart contracts, and digital platforms facilitate peer-to-peer energy transactions, promoting energy autonomy, community resilience, and local economic empowerment in SIDS.

7. Energy-Efficient Building Designs:

Energy-efficient building designs and green building standards are being adopted in SIDS to reduce energy consumption, improve indoor comfort, and lower utility bills. Passive design strategies, energy-efficient appliances, and renewable energy integration enhance building energy performance, resilience, and sustainability, while reducing carbon emissions and promoting climate adaptation in SIDS.

8. Community-Based Energy Initiatives:

Community-based energy initiatives empower local communities in SIDS to participate in energy decision-making, develop renewable energy projects, and benefit from clean energy solutions. Community-owned solar cooperatives, energy cooperatives, and shared microgrid systems foster social cohesion, economic empowerment, and energy resilience at the grassroots level, promoting inclusive and sustainable development in SIDS.

In summary, innovative solutions in energy production and distribution offer Small Island Developing States (SIDS) opportunities to overcome their energy challenges, enhance resilience, and accelerate the transition to sustainable and decentralized energy systems. By embracing technological innovations, fostering local partnerships, and promoting community engagement, SIDS can unlock the potential of clean energy to drive economic growth, environmental sustainability, and social equity in their communities.

5.4 Policy Frameworks for Sustainable Energy Development

Small Island Developing States (SIDS) are implementing comprehensive policy frameworks to support the transition to sustainable energy systems, address energy challenges, and achieve climate resilience and sustainability goals. This section explores the key policy approaches and initiatives adopted by SIDS to promote sustainable energy development.

1. Renewable Energy Targets and Strategies:

SIDS are setting ambitious renewable energy targets and developing long-term strategies to promote the deployment of renewable energy technologies. National renewable energy targets, such as the percentage of electricity generated from renewable sources by a certain year, provide a clear roadmap for scaling up renewable energy deployment and reducing dependence on imported fossil fuels.

2. Feed-in Tariffs and Incentive Mechanisms:

SIDS are implementing feed-in tariffs, feed-in premiums, and other incentive mechanisms to stimulate investment in renewable energy projects and attract private sector participation. Feed-in tariffs guarantee fixed prices for renewable energy generation, providing investors with stable returns and reducing financial risks associated with renewable energy projects in SIDS.

3. Energy Efficiency Standards and Regulations:

SIDS are adopting energy efficiency standards, labeling schemes, and building codes to promote energy conservation and efficiency in buildings, appliances, and industrial processes. Energy efficiency regulations mandate minimum energy performance standards for appliances, promote energy-efficient building designs, and incentivize energy-saving practices, reducing energy consumption and carbon emissions in SIDS.

4. Grid Modernization and Interconnection Policies:

SIDS are modernizing their electricity grids and implementing interconnection policies to integrate renewable energy sources, enhance grid stability, and improve energy reliability. Grid modernization initiatives, such as smart grid investments, grid expansion projects, and interconnection agreements with neighboring countries, enable SIDS to accommodate higher shares of variable renewable energy and optimize energy distribution.

5. Renewable Energy Financing Mechanisms:

SIDS are establishing renewable energy financing mechanisms, such as green banks, revolving funds, and concessional loans, to mobilize investment capital for renewable energy projects. Financial instruments, such as grants, concessional loans, and risk guarantees, de-risk investments, attract private sector capital, and catalyze renewable energy deployment in SIDS, especially in underserved and remote areas.

6. Energy Access Policies and Programs:

SIDS are implementing energy access policies and programs to expand electricity access to underserved communities, particularly in remote and off-grid areas. Off-grid electrification initiatives, decentralized energy solutions, and rural electrification programs provide affordable and reliable electricity services to marginalized populations, improving livelihoods, health outcomes, and quality of life in SIDS.

7. Climate Resilience and Disaster Preparedness:
SIDS are integrating climate resilience and disaster preparedness considerations into their energy policies and planning processes. Climate risk assessments, vulnerability assessments, and adaptation strategies inform energy infrastructure investments, resilience measures, and emergency response plans, ensuring that energy systems are resilient to climate change impacts and natural disasters in SIDS.

8. Multi-Stakeholder Engagement and Partnerships:
SIDS are fostering multi-stakeholder engagement and partnerships to mobilize resources, share expertise, and leverage collective efforts for sustainable energy development. Public-private partnerships, international cooperation initiatives, and civil society engagement platforms facilitate knowledge exchange, technology transfer, and capacity-building for renewable energy deployment in SIDS.

In summary, robust policy frameworks are essential for accelerating the transition to sustainable energy systems in Small Island Developing States (SIDS). By implementing renewable energy targets, incentivizing investment, promoting energy efficiency, and integrating climate resilience considerations, SIDS can advance towards a sustainable energy future that enhances energy security, promotes economic growth, and safeguards environmental integrity in their communities.

In conclusion, transitioning to sustainable energy sources is imperative for SIDS to achieve energy security, mitigate climate change, and promote inclusive and sustainable development. Through innovative solutions, supportive policies, and international collaboration, SIDS can overcome energy challenges and unlock the potential of renewable resources to power their future.

Chapter – 6

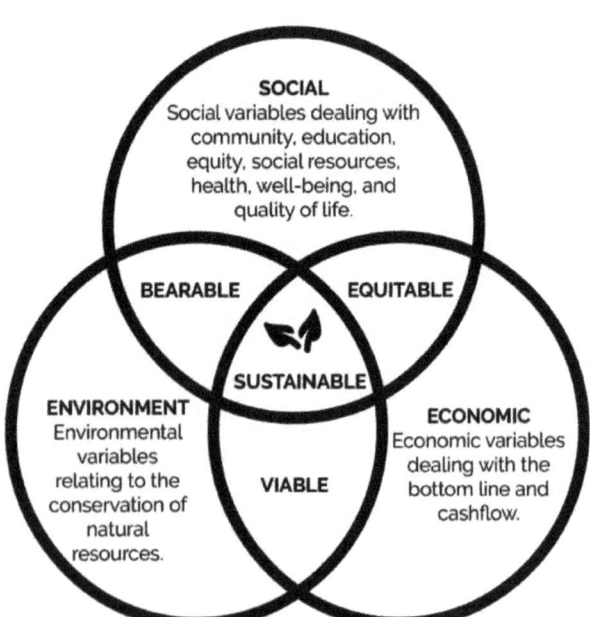

Sustainable Tourism and Economic Diversification

Small Island Developing States (SIDS) often rely heavily on tourism as a significant driver of economic growth and development. However, the sustainability of this industry is crucial for preserving the natural environment, cultural heritage, and social fabric of these island nations. This chapter explores the importance of tourism in SIDS economies, the need to balance economic growth with environmental preservation, community-based tourism initiatives, and the promotion of cultural heritage through sustainable tourism practices.

6.1 Importance of Tourism in SIDS Economies

Tourism plays a pivotal role in the economies of Small Island Developing States (SIDS), serving as a major driver of economic growth, employment generation, and foreign exchange earnings. This section explores the significance of tourism in SIDS economies, highlighting its contributions, opportunities, and challenges.

1. Economic Contribution:

Tourism is a significant contributor to the gross domestic product (GDP) of SIDS, generating revenue through visitor expenditures, accommodation services, transportation, and recreational activities. The tourism sector supports a wide range of industries, including hospitality, transportation, food and beverage, retail, and cultural services, driving economic diversification and job creation in SIDS economies.

2. Employment Opportunities:

Tourism is a major source of employment in SIDS, providing job opportunities for a significant portion of the local workforce, including youth, women, and rural communities. Employment in the tourism sector encompasses a diverse range of roles, such as hotel staff, tour guides, artisans, taxi drivers, and service providers, contributing to poverty reduction, social inclusion, and human capital development in SIDS.

3. Foreign Exchange Earnings:

Tourism generates foreign exchange earnings for SIDS economies through visitor spending on accommodation, dining, shopping, and recreational activities. Tourism receipts contribute to the balance of payments, support import-dependent economies, and strengthen external resilience to external shocks, such as fluctuations in commodity prices and exchange rates, in SIDS.

4. Infrastructure Development:

Tourism drives infrastructure development in SIDS, catalyzing investments in transportation networks, airport facilities, seaports, roads, telecommunications, and public utilities. Infrastructure upgrades and expansions enhance accessibility, connectivity, and quality of tourism services, attracting visitors, stimulating business growth, and improving the overall competitiveness of SIDS destinations.

5. Cultural Preservation and Heritage Conservation:

Tourism promotes cultural preservation and heritage conservation in SIDS, showcasing the rich cultural traditions, customs, and indigenous knowledge of local communities. Cultural tourism initiatives, such as heritage tours, cultural festivals, and craft markets, support the revitalization of traditional practices, arts, and crafts, preserving cultural identity and promoting intercultural exchange in SIDS.

6. Environmental Conservation and Sustainable Development:

Tourism fosters environmental conservation and sustainable development in SIDS by raising awareness of environmental issues, promoting conservation initiatives, and supporting eco-friendly practices. Sustainable tourism practices, such as nature-based tourism, wildlife conservation, and marine protected areas, contribute to biodiversity conservation, ecosystem preservation, and climate resilience in SIDS.

7. Community Empowerment and Socio-Economic Benefits:

Tourism empowers local communities in SIDS by providing opportunities for entrepreneurship, small business development, and income generation. Community-based tourism initiatives, homestay programs, and cultural experiences enable communities to participate in tourism value chains, retain ownership of tourism assets, and benefit directly from tourism revenues, fostering social inclusion and equitable development in SIDS.

8. Tourism Resilience and Crisis Management:

Tourism resilience is a critical consideration for SIDS, given their vulnerability to natural disasters, climate change impacts, and global crises. Diversification of tourism markets, risk management strategies, and crisis preparedness plans help SIDS mitigate the impacts of external shocks, maintain tourism competitiveness, and recover quickly from disruptions, safeguarding livelihoods and economic stability.

In summary, tourism plays a multifaceted role in the economies of Small Island Developing States (SIDS), contributing to economic growth, employment generation, foreign exchange earnings, infrastructure development, cultural preservation, environmental conservation, community empowerment, and resilience building. By harnessing the potential of tourism in a sustainable and inclusive manner, SIDS can maximize the socio-economic benefits of tourism while preserving their natural and cultural heritage for future generations.

6.2 Balancing Economic Growth with Environmental Preservation

Sustainable tourism development in SIDS requires striking a delicate balance between economic growth and environmental preservation:

- **Sustainable Tourism Planning:** SIDS develop comprehensive tourism master plans and policies that integrate environmental, social, and economic considerations, promote responsible tourism practices, and ensure the long-term viability of tourism destinations.

- **Environmental Conservation:** SIDS implement measures to protect and preserve natural habitats, biodiversity, and ecosystems, including establishing marine protected areas, regulating coastal development, and promoting sustainable land use practices.

- **Sustainable Infrastructure:** SIDS invest in sustainable tourism infrastructure that minimizes environmental impacts, incorporates green building principles, utilizes renewable energy sources, and adopts water and waste management practices.

- **Sustainable Transport:** SIDS promote sustainable transportation options for tourists, such as public transit, cycling, and walking, to reduce carbon emissions, alleviate traffic congestion, and enhance the visitor experience.

By adopting sustainable tourism practices, SIDS can maximize the economic benefits of tourism while safeguarding their natural and cultural heritage for future generations.

In Small Island Developing States (SIDS), the pursuit of economic growth through tourism is often intertwined with the imperative of environmental preservation. This section examines the delicate balance between economic development and environmental conservation in SIDS, exploring strategies to ensure sustainable tourism practices while safeguarding fragile ecosystems and natural resources.

1. Sustainable Tourism Development:

Sustainable tourism development is essential for balancing economic growth with environmental preservation in SIDS. Adopting principles of sustainable tourism, such as minimizing environmental impacts, conserving natural resources, respecting local cultures, and benefiting local communities, promotes responsible tourism practices that support long-term economic, social, and environmental sustainability in SIDS.

2. Ecosystem-Based Management:

Ecosystem-based management approaches prioritize the conservation and sustainable use of natural resources in tourism development planning and decision-making processes. Protecting sensitive ecosystems, such as coral reefs, mangroves, and terrestrial habitats, ensures biodiversity conservation, enhances ecosystem resilience, and maintains the integrity of natural landscapes in SIDS destinations.

3. Carrying Capacity Assessment:

Carrying capacity assessments help determine the maximum number of visitors that a destination can sustainably accommodate without compromising environmental quality, cultural integrity, and visitor experience. By establishing limits on tourism activities, managing visitor flows, and implementing visitor management strategies, SIDS can prevent overdevelopment, congestion, and environmental degradation in tourism hotspots.

4. Environmental Impact Assessment (EIA):

Environmental impact assessments (EIAs) evaluate the potential environmental, social, and cultural impacts of tourism development projects before they are approved and implemented. Conducting EIAs ensures that tourism developments comply with environmental regulations, mitigate adverse impacts, and incorporate measures to protect sensitive habitats, wildlife, and cultural heritage sites in SIDS.

5. Sustainable Infrastructure Development:

Sustainable infrastructure development practices promote energy efficiency, water conservation, waste management, and green building standards in tourism facilities and infrastructure projects. Implementing sustainable design principles, such as renewable energy systems, rainwater harvesting, wastewater treatment, and low-impact construction techniques, minimizes environmental footprints and enhances resilience in SIDS.

6. Ecotourism and Nature-Based Tourism:

Ecotourism and nature-based tourism initiatives emphasize nature conservation, environmental education, and community involvement in tourism activities. Promoting ecotourism experiences, such as wildlife viewing, nature walks, and cultural exchanges, encourages responsible tourism behavior, supports local conservation efforts, and generates economic benefits for communities while preserving natural ecosystems in SIDS.

7. Marine and Coastal Management:

Marine and coastal management strategies focus on protecting marine biodiversity, managing coastal development, and mitigating human impacts on marine ecosystems in SIDS. Implementing marine protected areas, sustainable fishing practices, coral reef restoration projects, and coastal zoning regulations safeguard marine resources, enhance resilience to climate change, and support sustainable fisheries and tourism livelihoods.

8. Education and Awareness:

Education and awareness-raising initiatives play a crucial role in fostering a culture of environmental stewardship and responsible tourism behavior among tourists, industry stakeholders, and local communities in SIDS. Environmental education programs, interpretive signage, and community outreach activities raise awareness of conservation issues, promote sustainable lifestyles, and empower stakeholders to participate in sustainable tourism practices in SIDS.

In summary, balancing economic growth with environmental preservation in Small Island Developing States (SIDS) requires a holistic approach that integrates sustainable tourism practices, ecosystem-based management, carrying capacity assessments, environmental impact assessments, sustainable infrastructure development, ecotourism initiatives, marine and coastal management strategies, and education and awareness-raising efforts. By embracing sustainable tourism principles and fostering partnerships among stakeholders, SIDS can achieve a harmonious balance between tourism development and environmental conservation, ensuring the long-term sustainability of their natural and cultural assets.

6.3 Community-Based Tourism Initiatives

Community-based tourism initiatives empower local communities to actively participate in tourism development, share in the benefits, and preserve their cultural and natural heritage. In Small Island Developing States (SIDS), community-based tourism plays a vital role in fostering sustainable tourism practices, supporting grassroots entrepreneurship, and promoting socio-economic development. This section explores the principles, benefits, and challenges of community-based tourism initiatives in SIDS.

1. Principles of Community-Based Tourism:

Community-based tourism is guided by principles of community ownership, participation, empowerment, and sustainability. It prioritizes the involvement of local communities in decision-making processes, respects cultural traditions and values, promotes equitable distribution of benefits, and fosters environmental stewardship and conservation in tourism activities.

2. Empowerment of Local Communities:

Community-based tourism initiatives empower local communities in SIDS by providing opportunities for economic diversification, income generation, and livelihood enhancement. Through tourism-related businesses, such as homestays, craft cooperatives, tour guiding services, and cultural experiences, communities can leverage their unique assets, skills, and knowledge to create sustainable livelihoods and improve living standards.

3. Preservation of Cultural Heritage:

Community-based tourism initiatives promote the preservation and celebration of cultural heritage and traditions in SIDS. Indigenous knowledge, traditional crafts, music, dance, storytelling, and culinary traditions are showcased through authentic cultural experiences, cultural immersion programs, and community-led tours, fostering cultural pride, identity, and intercultural exchange.

4. Conservation of Natural Resources:

Community-based tourism initiatives contribute to the conservation of natural resources and ecosystems in SIDS by promoting responsible tourism practices and supporting conservation initiatives. Community-managed protected areas, nature-based tourism activities, and eco-friendly accommodations prioritize environmental sustainability, reduce ecological footprints, and protect fragile ecosystems, such as coral reefs, mangroves, and rainforests.

5. Socio-Economic Benefits for Communities:

Community-based tourism initiatives generate socio-economic benefits for local communities in SIDS, including employment opportunities, income generation, and capacity-building. Revenue generated from tourism activities is reinvested in community development projects, such as education, healthcare, infrastructure, and environmental conservation, enhancing social welfare and resilience in SIDS communities.

6. Authentic and Responsible Tourism Experiences:

Community-based tourism offers authentic and immersive experiences for travelers seeking meaningful interactions with local cultures and communities. Homestays, cultural exchanges, community-led tours, and participatory activities provide travelers with opportunities to engage with local traditions, customs, and lifestyles, fostering cross-cultural understanding, respect, and appreciation.

7. Challenges and Considerations:

Community-based tourism initiatives face challenges in SIDS, including limited access to market opportunities, capacity constraints, lack of infrastructure, and vulnerability to external shocks, such as natural disasters and global crises. Addressing these challenges requires capacity-building, market development, sustainable financing mechanisms, and partnerships with tourism stakeholders and government agencies.

8. Partnerships and Collaboration:

Partnerships and collaboration among stakeholders are essential for the success of community-based tourism initiatives in SIDS. Engaging local communities, tourism operators, government agencies, non-governmental organizations, and international development partners fosters collective action, resource mobilization, and knowledge-sharing, enabling sustainable tourism development that benefits both communities and visitors.

In summary, community-based tourism initiatives offer Small Island Developing States (SIDS) an inclusive and sustainable approach to tourism development that empowers local communities, preserves cultural and natural heritage, and promotes responsible tourism practices. By embracing community ownership, participation, and collaboration, SIDS can harness the potential of tourism as a tool for socio-economic development, cultural preservation, and environmental conservation in their communities.

6.4 Promoting Cultural Heritage and Sustainable Tourism Practices

Sustainable tourism practices in SIDS prioritize the protection and promotion of cultural heritage:

- **Cultural Preservation:** SIDS safeguard their cultural heritage, including indigenous traditions, languages, rituals, folklore, and historic sites, from commodification, distortion, and exploitation by tourists and commercial interests.

- **Heritage Interpretation:** Sustainable tourism initiatives incorporate heritage interpretation programs, guided tours, storytelling sessions, and cultural exchanges that educate tourists about the significance of local customs, beliefs, and practices, fostering respect and appreciation for diverse cultures.

- **Cultural Festivals and Events:** SIDS organize cultural festivals, celebrations, and events that showcase traditional music, dance, art, cuisine, and craftsmanship, providing opportunities for cultural expression, intercultural dialogue, and community engagement.

- **Sustainable Souvenirs:** SIDS promote the production and sale of sustainable souvenirs made from locally sourced materials, such as handicrafts, textiles, pottery, and artwork, supporting local artisans, preserving traditional craftsmanship, and reducing environmental impacts.

By integrating cultural heritage into tourism experiences, SIDS can differentiate themselves in the global tourism market, enhance visitor satisfaction, and create memorable and authentic travel experiences.

In Small Island Developing States (SIDS), the preservation and promotion of cultural heritage are integral to sustainable tourism practices. This section explores the importance of cultural heritage in tourism development and highlights strategies for promoting sustainable tourism practices that respect and celebrate the unique cultural identities of SIDS.

1. Cultural Heritage as Tourism Assets:

Cultural heritage, including traditional customs, rituals, folklore, arts, cuisine, and architecture, serves as a valuable tourism asset in SIDS. Preserving and showcasing cultural heritage attractions, such as historic sites, museums, cultural festivals, and performing arts, enriches the tourism experience, attracts visitors, and fosters cultural exchange and appreciation.

2. Authentic Cultural Experiences:

Promoting authentic cultural experiences is essential for sustainable tourism development in SIDS. Offering immersive activities, such as cultural tours, workshops, demonstrations, and cultural performances, allows visitors to engage with local communities, learn about traditional practices, and gain insights into indigenous cultures, fostering cross-cultural understanding and respect.

3. Community Engagement and Empowerment:

Engaging local communities in tourism planning, decision-making, and benefit-sharing processes is fundamental to sustainable tourism practices in SIDS. Community-based tourism initiatives, participatory tourism planning, and revenue-sharing mechanisms ensure that communities have a stake in tourism development, derive socio-economic benefits, and retain ownership of their cultural heritage assets.

4. Cultural Preservation and Conservation:

Cultural preservation and conservation efforts are essential for safeguarding the integrity and authenticity of cultural heritage in SIDS. Heritage conservation measures, such as restoration projects, conservation workshops, and heritage management plans, protect historic sites, artifacts, and traditions from degradation, vandalism, and over-commercialization, ensuring their long-term viability as tourism attractions.

5. Sustainable Tourism Management:

Implementing sustainable tourism management practices is critical for minimizing negative impacts on cultural heritage and local communities in SIDS. Sustainable tourism certification programs, visitor codes of conduct, and carrying capacity assessments help regulate tourism activities, mitigate overcrowding, and preserve the integrity of cultural sites, ensuring that tourism development is environmentally, socially, and culturally sustainable.

6. Cultural Interpretation and Education:

Cultural interpretation and education initiatives enhance visitor understanding and appreciation of cultural heritage in SIDS. Interpretive signage, guided tours, educational programs, and cultural exchanges provide visitors with insights into local customs, traditions, and history, fostering respect for cultural diversity, promoting responsible tourism behavior, and encouraging cultural immersion experiences.

7. Integration of Traditional Knowledge:
Integrating traditional knowledge systems into tourism development practices enriches the authenticity and sustainability of cultural tourism experiences in SIDS. Indigenous storytelling, traditional crafts, medicinal plant tours, and culinary experiences offer opportunities to showcase indigenous knowledge, skills, and practices, while promoting cultural pride, identity, and intergenerational learning.

8. Destination Branding and Marketing:
Destination branding and marketing strategies highlight the cultural heritage and authenticity of SIDS as unique selling propositions in the global tourism market. Promoting cultural festivals, heritage trails, cultural routes, and indigenous tourism experiences in marketing campaigns attracts culturally curious travelers, enhances destination competitiveness, and supports sustainable tourism development in SIDS.

In summary, promoting cultural heritage and sustainable tourism practices in Small Island Developing States (SIDS) is essential for preserving cultural identity, fostering community empowerment, and achieving long-term tourism sustainability. By embracing cultural heritage as a tourism asset and integrating sustainable tourism principles into destination management, SIDS can leverage their unique cultural heritage to create memorable and meaningful tourism experiences while safeguarding cultural and natural resources for future generations.

In summary, sustainable tourism development in SIDS entails balancing economic growth with environmental preservation, empowering local communities, and promoting cultural heritage through responsible tourism practices. By adopting a holistic approach to tourism planning and management, SIDS can maximize the benefits of tourism while safeguarding their natural and cultural assets for future generations.

Chapter – 7

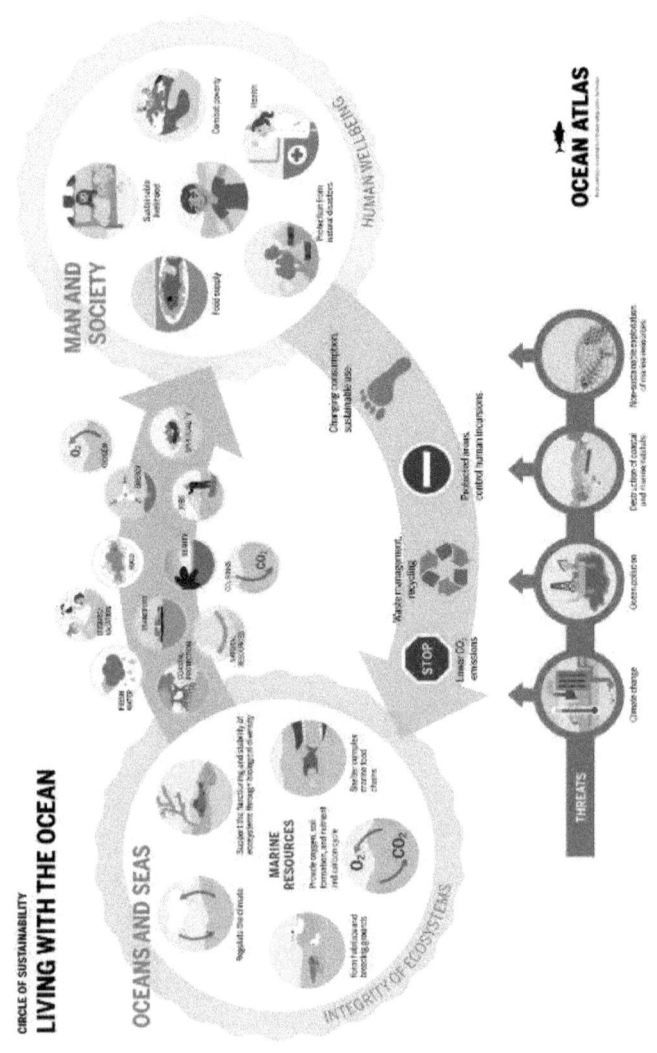

Ocean Conservation and Marine Resources Management

The oceans are integral to the identity, economy, and well-being of Small Island Developing States (SIDS). This chapter explores the opportunities presented by the blue economy, the challenges of overfishing and the importance of sustainable fisheries management, the conservation of marine protected areas and coral reefs, and the sustainable harnessing of marine resources.

7.1 Blue Economy Opportunities

The blue economy presents numerous opportunities for SIDS to achieve sustainable development while conserving marine ecosystems:

- **Fisheries and Aquaculture:** SIDS can capitalize on their rich marine biodiversity to develop sustainable fisheries and aquaculture industries, providing food security, employment, and economic growth.

- **Tourism and Recreation:** SIDS can leverage their pristine coastal and marine environments to attract tourists interested in diving, snorkeling, sailing, and eco-tourism, generating revenue and promoting conservation.

- **Renewable Energy:** SIDS can harness ocean energy resources, such as tidal, wave, and offshore wind energy, to diversify their energy mix, reduce reliance on imported fossil fuels, and mitigate climate change.

- **Biotechnology and Pharmaceuticals:** SIDS possess unique marine biodiversity with potential applications in biotechnology, pharmaceuticals, and marine bioproducts, offering opportunities for scientific research, innovation, and economic development.

- **Marine Transportation and Trade:** SIDS strategic maritime location provides opportunities for maritime transportation, shipping services, and port development, facilitating international trade and connectivity.

By embracing the blue economy concept, SIDS can unlock the economic potential of their marine resources while promoting sustainability and resilience.

The concept of the blue economy encompasses the sustainable use of ocean resources to foster economic growth, improve livelihoods, and promote environmental sustainability. In Small Island Developing States (SIDS), the blue economy offers unique opportunities for harnessing the potential of marine and coastal resources to drive socio-economic development. This section explores the diverse opportunities presented by the blue economy in SIDS and examines strategies for maximizing its benefits while ensuring the conservation and sustainable management of marine ecosystems.

1. Fisheries and Aquaculture:

Fisheries and aquaculture are key pillars of the blue economy in SIDS, providing livelihoods for coastal communities and contributing to food security and economic growth. Sustainable fisheries management practices, responsible aquaculture development, and value-added processing activities unlock the economic potential of marine resources while safeguarding fish stocks, biodiversity, and marine habitats.

2. Marine Tourism and Recreation:

Marine tourism and recreation activities, such as snorkeling, diving, sailing, and wildlife watching, are important drivers of the blue economy in SIDS. Pristine coral reefs, clear waters, and diverse marine life attract visitors seeking immersive nature experiences, supporting tourism businesses, creating jobs, and generating revenue for local economies while promoting conservation and sustainable use of marine resources.

3. Coastal Infrastructure and Blue Infrastructure Development:

Investments in coastal infrastructure and blue infrastructure projects, such as ports, harbors, marinas, coastal protection structures, and marine transportation networks, stimulate economic growth, enhance connectivity, and facilitate trade and commerce in SIDS. Sustainable infrastructure development practices prioritize resilience, adaptation to climate change, and conservation of coastal ecosystems, ensuring long-term sustainability and prosperity.

4. Renewable Energy from Marine Resources:

Renewable energy from marine resources, including offshore wind, tidal energy, wave energy, and ocean thermal energy conversion (OTEC), presents opportunities for clean energy generation and energy security in SIDS. Marine renewable energy projects harness the power of ocean currents, waves, and tides to produce electricity, reduce dependency on fossil fuels, and mitigate greenhouse gas emissions, contributing to climate resilience and sustainability.

5. Marine Biotechnology and Pharmaceuticals:

Marine biotechnology and pharmaceutical research offer promising avenues for innovation and economic diversification in SIDS. Bioprospecting marine organisms for bioactive compounds, enzymes, and pharmaceutical products holds potential for developing new treatments for diseases, improving agricultural productivity, and creating value-added products from marine resources, driving economic growth and scientific advancement.

6. Sustainable Fisheries Value Chains:

Building sustainable fisheries value chains enhances the economic viability and resilience of the blue economy in SIDS. Investing in fish processing, cold storage facilities, transportation infrastructure, and market linkages improves post-harvest handling, value addition, and market access for fishery products, enhancing income opportunities for fishers, supporting small-scale enterprises, and promoting sustainable seafood consumption.

7. Marine Conservation and Ecotourism:

Marine conservation and ecotourism initiatives contribute to the blue economy by preserving biodiversity, protecting critical habitats, and promoting sustainable tourism practices in SIDS. Marine protected areas, coral reef conservation projects, and ecotourism ventures offer opportunities for nature-based tourism, environmental education, and research collaborations, generating revenue while safeguarding marine ecosystems.

8. Blue Finance and Investment Opportunities:

Blue finance mechanisms, such as green bonds, sustainable fisheries funds, and blue economy investment platforms, mobilize capital for blue economy projects and initiatives in SIDS. Blended finance models, public-private partnerships, and innovative financing mechanisms leverage public and private sector resources to support sustainable ocean investments, unlock economic opportunities, and address marine conservation challenges.

In summary, the blue economy presents diverse opportunities for sustainable development and economic resilience in Small Island Developing States (SIDS). By harnessing the potential of marine and coastal resources through responsible management, innovation, and strategic partnerships, SIDS can unlock the economic, social, and environmental benefits of the blue economy while safeguarding the health and integrity of marine ecosystems for future generations.

7.2 Overfishing and Sustainable Fisheries Management

Overfishing and unsustainable fishing practices threaten the health of marine ecosystems and the livelihoods of coastal communities in SIDS:

- **Stock Depletion:** Overfishing leads to the depletion of fish stocks, loss of biodiversity, and ecosystem imbalance, jeopardizing the long-term sustainability of fisheries and marine resources.

- **Illegal, Unreported, and Unregulated (IUU) Fishing:** IUU fishing undermines fisheries management efforts, compromises food security, and deprives legitimate fishers of income, posing challenges for enforcement and governance.

- **Bycatch and Habitat Destruction:** Unsustainable fishing practices, such as bottom trawling and ghost fishing gear, result in high levels of bycatch, habitat destruction, and ecosystem degradation, threatening marine biodiversity and ecosystem services.

To address these challenges, SIDS implement sustainable fisheries management measures, including:

- **Fisheries Regulations:** SIDS enact fisheries regulations, quotas, and licensing schemes to limit fishing effort, protect vulnerable species, and prevent overexploitation of fish stocks.

- **Monitoring and Surveillance:** SIDS invest in monitoring, control, and surveillance (MCS) systems to detect and deter illegal fishing activities, enhance compliance with fisheries regulations, and improve data collection and reporting.

- **Marine Spatial Planning:** SIDS adopt marine spatial planning (MSP) approaches to allocate fishing zones, designate marine protected areas, and minimize conflicts between fishing activities and other marine uses, promoting ecosystem-based management and stakeholder participation.

- **Community-Based Fisheries Management**: SIDS engage local communities in co-management arrangements, participatory decision-making processes, and sustainable fishing practices, empowering fishers as stewards of marine resources and enhancing social equity and resilience.

By adopting a holistic approach to fisheries management, SIDS can conserve marine biodiversity, ensure food security, and sustainably manage their fisheries for future generations.

Overfishing poses a significant threat to marine biodiversity, food security, and livelihoods in Small Island Developing States (SIDS). Sustainable fisheries management is essential for ensuring the long-term viability of marine resources and the economic prosperity of coastal communities. This section examines the challenges of overfishing in SIDS and explores strategies for promoting sustainable fisheries management practices.

1. Overfishing and Depletion of Fish Stocks:

Overfishing, driven by excessive fishing pressure, destructive fishing practices, and illegal, unreported, and unregulated (IUU) fishing activities, depletes fish stocks, undermines ecosystem health, and threatens marine biodiversity in SIDS. Unsustainable fishing practices, such as overcapacity, bycatch, and habitat destruction, jeopardize the resilience of marine ecosystems and the sustainability of fisheries resources.

2. Impacts on Food Security and Livelihoods:

Overfishing has profound implications for food security, nutrition, and livelihoods in SIDS, where fish often constitute a primary source of protein, income, and employment for coastal communities. Declines in fish stocks reduce fish availability, increase food prices, and jeopardize the livelihoods of small-scale fishers, fish processors, and seafood traders, exacerbating poverty and vulnerability in SIDS.

3. Sustainable Fisheries Management Principles:

Sustainable fisheries management principles, such as the precautionary approach, ecosystem-based management, and rights-based fisheries management, provide a framework for addressing overfishing and promoting the sustainable use of marine resources in SIDS. Implementing science-based fisheries assessments, setting catch limits, and enforcing regulations help maintain fish stocks at sustainable levels and restore depleted populations.

4. Fisheries Regulations and Enforcement:

Strengthening fisheries regulations and enhancing enforcement mechanisms are critical for combating overfishing and IUU fishing activities in SIDS. Implementing catch quotas, size limits, gear restrictions, and marine protected areas (MPAs) helps regulate fishing activities, reduce overexploitation, and protect vulnerable species and habitats from unsustainable practices.

5. Community-Based Fisheries Management:

Community-based fisheries management approaches empower local communities to participate in decision-making processes, monitor fish stocks, and enforce fisheries regulations at the grassroots level. Collaborative fisheries management initiatives, such as co-management agreements, community fishery councils, and territorial use rights for fisheries (TURFs), promote stewardship, ownership, and compliance with sustainable fishing practices in SIDS.

6. Ecosystem-Based Fisheries Management:

Ecosystem-based fisheries management (EBFM) integrates ecological, social, and economic considerations into fisheries management decisions, aiming to maintain ecosystem integrity and resilience while supporting sustainable fisheries. EBFM approaches, such as marine spatial planning, ecosystem modeling, and ecosystem-based harvest strategies, ensure that fisheries management measures account for ecosystem dynamics, biodiversity conservation, and ecosystem services in SIDS.

7. Market-Based Fisheries Management:

Market-based fisheries management mechanisms, such as certification schemes, eco-labeling programs, and traceability systems, incentivize sustainable fishing practices and promote market access for responsibly sourced seafood products in SIDS. Adopting sustainable seafood standards, such as Marine Stewardship Council (MSC) certification, enhances market credibility, consumer confidence, and economic opportunities for fisheries stakeholders.

8. International Cooperation and Regional Fisheries Management Organizations (RFMOs):

International cooperation and collaboration through regional fisheries management organizations (RFMOs) are essential for addressing transboundary fisheries issues, managing shared fish stocks, and combating IUU fishing in SIDS. Participating in RFMOs, negotiating bilateral agreements, and sharing fisheries data and information facilitate coordinated action, harmonized regulations, and collective efforts to conserve and sustainably manage fisheries resources in SIDS.

In summary, overfishing poses significant challenges to marine ecosystems, food security, and livelihoods in Small Island Developing States (SIDS). By adopting sustainable fisheries management practices, strengthening regulations, empowering local communities, and promoting international cooperation, SIDS can mitigate the impacts of overfishing, restore fish stocks, and ensure the long-term sustainability of fisheries resources for present and future generations.

7.3 Marine Protected Areas and Coral Reef Conservation

Marine protected areas (MPAs) play a critical role in conserving marine biodiversity and ecosystem services in SIDS:

- **Biodiversity Hotspots:** MPAs protect vulnerable habitats, critical breeding grounds, and endangered species, safeguarding marine biodiversity and genetic diversity.

- **Ecosystem Resilience:** MPAs enhance ecosystem resilience to climate change impacts, such as ocean warming, acidification, and sea-level rise, by providing refuge areas for species and promoting habitat connectivity.

- **Sustainable Fisheries:** MPAs serve as replenishment zones for fish stocks, spillover areas for fishing grounds, and natural nurseries for juvenile fish, supporting sustainable fisheries and enhancing fishery yields.

- **Tourism and Recreation:** MPAs attract eco-tourists, divers, and snorkelers interested in exploring pristine marine environments, generating revenue for local communities and supporting conservation efforts.

- **Cultural Heritage:** MPAs preserve cultural heritage sites, traditional fishing grounds, and sacred areas, maintaining cultural identity and spiritual connections to the sea for indigenous communities.

SIDS prioritize coral reef conservation as a cornerstone of marine biodiversity conservation and sustainable development:

- **Coral Reefs:** Coral reefs are biodiversity hotspots that support a quarter of marine species, provide coastal protection, and generate significant economic value through tourism, fisheries, and shoreline stabilization.

- **Threats to Coral Reefs:** Coral reefs face numerous threats, including overfishing, pollution, habitat destruction, sedimentation, coral bleaching, and ocean acidification, exacerbated by climate change impacts such as rising sea temperatures and extreme weather events.

- **Coral Reef Management:** SIDS implement coral reef management strategies, including coral reef monitoring, restoration, and rehabilitation programs, to mitigate threats, enhance reef resilience, and promote ecosystem recovery.

By establishing and effectively managing MPAs and conserving coral reefs, SIDS can safeguard marine biodiversity, support sustainable fisheries, and promote ecotourism while enhancing resilience to climate change.

Marine Protected Areas (MPAs) play a crucial role in conserving marine biodiversity, preserving ecosystems, and promoting sustainable fisheries in Small Island Developing States (SIDS). Coral reefs, in particular, are vital marine ecosystems that support biodiversity, provide ecosystem services, and contribute to coastal resilience. This section explores the importance of MPAs and coral reef conservation efforts in SIDS, as well as strategies for enhancing their effectiveness.

1. Importance of Marine Protected Areas:

Marine Protected Areas (MPAs) are designated areas where human activities are regulated to conserve marine biodiversity, protect critical habitats, and sustainably manage fisheries. MPAs serve as refuges for endangered species, nurseries for fish larvae, and spawning grounds for commercially valuable species, contributing to the resilience and productivity of marine ecosystems in SIDS.

2. Coral Reef Ecosystems:

Coral reef ecosystems are among the most biodiverse and economically valuable ecosystems on the planet, providing habitat for a quarter of all marine species, supporting fisheries, and protecting coastlines from erosion and storm surges. Coral reefs also provide ecosystem services, such as food, income, recreation, and cultural significance, to coastal communities in SIDS, making their conservation essential for sustainable development.

3. Threats to Coral Reefs:

Coral reefs face numerous threats in SIDS, including overfishing, destructive fishing practices, habitat degradation, pollution, coastal development, climate change, and ocean acidification. Human activities, such as dynamite fishing, coral mining, sedimentation, and nutrient runoff, degrade coral reef health, reduce biodiversity, and diminish ecosystem resilience, jeopardizing the long-term survival of coral reefs in SIDS.

4. Marine Protected Areas for Coral Reef Conservation:

Marine Protected Areas (MPAs) are effective tools for conserving coral reef ecosystems and enhancing their resilience to anthropogenic and environmental threats. Establishing MPAs with zoning regulations, no-take zones, and buffer areas helps protect coral reefs from overexploitation, habitat destruction, and pollution, while promoting sustainable fishing practices, scientific research, and ecotourism activities in SIDS.

5. Coral Reef Monitoring and Research:

Monitoring and research initiatives are essential for assessing coral reef health, understanding ecosystem dynamics, and identifying conservation priorities in SIDS. Monitoring programs, such as coral reef surveys, water quality monitoring, and biodiversity assessments, provide data on coral reef condition, population trends, and environmental stressors, informing management decisions and adaptive management strategies for MPAs.

6. Community Engagement and Stakeholder Participation:

Engaging local communities, stakeholders, and indigenous groups in MPA planning, management, and enforcement enhances the effectiveness and legitimacy of conservation efforts in SIDS. Participatory approaches, community-based monitoring, and traditional ecological knowledge facilitate collaboration, foster stewardship, and build resilience among coastal communities, strengthening the social foundation for MPA management and coral reef conservation.

7. Climate Resilience and Adaptation Strategies:

Climate resilience and adaptation strategies are essential for safeguarding coral reefs and MPAs from the impacts of climate change, such as rising sea temperatures, coral bleaching, and ocean acidification. Implementing climate-smart management practices, such as coral reef restoration, species translocations, and ecosystem-based adaptation measures, enhances the resilience of coral reefs and MPAs to climate stressors, enabling them to persist and thrive in changing environments.

8. International Cooperation and Funding Mechanisms:

International cooperation and funding mechanisms play a crucial role in supporting MPA establishment, coral reef conservation, and capacity-building efforts in SIDS. Global initiatives, such as the International Coral Reef Initiative (ICRI), the Coral Triangle Initiative (CTI), and the Global Environment Facility (GEF), provide technical assistance, financial support, and knowledge exchange platforms to strengthen MPA networks, enhance coral reef resilience, and promote sustainable development in SIDS.

In summary, Marine Protected Areas (MPAs) and coral reef conservation efforts are essential for safeguarding marine biodiversity, preserving ecosystem services, and promoting sustainable fisheries in Small Island Developing States (SIDS). By establishing MPAs, engaging local communities, implementing adaptive management strategies, and fostering international collaboration, SIDS can conserve coral reef ecosystems and ensure their resilience in the face of global environmental challenges.

7.4 Harnessing Marine Resources Sustainably

SIDS explore opportunities to harness marine resources sustainably for economic development while minimizing environmental impacts:

- **Sustainable Aquaculture:** SIDS promote sustainable aquaculture practices, such as integrated multi-trophic aquaculture (IMTA), recirculating aquaculture systems (RAS), and land-based aquaponics, to produce seafood while reducing pressure on wild fish stocks and minimizing environmental impacts.

- **Seaweed Cultivation:** SIDS cultivate seaweed species for various applications, including food, feed, cosmetics, pharmaceuticals, and biofuel production, offering economic opportunities while providing ecosystem services such as carbon sequestration and nutrient cycling.

- **Deep-Sea Mining:** SIDS explore the potential of deep-sea mining for rare earth minerals, polymetallic nodules, and hydrothermal vents, balancing economic benefits with environmental risks and ensuring responsible mining practices to prevent habitat destruction and ecosystem disturbance.

- **Marine Biotechnology:** SIDS invest in marine biotechnology research and innovation to discover new bioproducts, biomaterials, and pharmaceutical compounds with commercial applications, fostering economic diversification and technological advancement.

By harnessing marine resources sustainably, SIDS can support economic growth, create employment opportunities, and promote innovation while safeguarding marine ecosystems and biodiversity for future generations.

Harnessing marine resources sustainably is essential for promoting economic development, ensuring food security, and conserving biodiversity in Small Island Developing States (SIDS). This section explores the diverse array of marine resources found in SIDS waters and examines strategies for their sustainable management and utilization.

1. Fisheries Resources:

Fisheries resources are a vital component of marine ecosystems and provide a critical source of protein, income, and livelihoods for coastal communities in SIDS. Sustainable fisheries management practices, such as setting catch limits, regulating fishing gear, and enforcing conservation measures, are essential for maintaining fish stocks at sustainable levels and supporting the long-term viability of fisheries resources.

2. Aquaculture:

Aquaculture, or fish farming, offers opportunities for diversifying food production, increasing seafood supply, and reducing pressure on wild fish stocks in SIDS. Sustainable aquaculture practices, such as site selection, water quality management, disease control, and feed optimization, minimize environmental impacts and ensure the ecological sustainability of aquaculture operations in SIDS.

3. Seaweed Farming:

Seaweed farming is an emerging industry in SIDS that offers economic benefits, environmental benefits, and opportunities for sustainable livelihoods. Seaweed cultivation provides a source of income for coastal communities, improves water quality through nutrient uptake, sequesters carbon dioxide from the atmosphere, and enhances coastal resilience to climate change impacts, such as ocean acidification and sea-level rise.

4. Marine Biotechnology:

Marine biotechnology holds promise for unlocking the potential of marine resources for pharmaceuticals, bioproducts, and bioenergy in SIDS. Bioprospecting marine organisms for bioactive compounds, enzymes, and genetic resources offers opportunities for developing new medicines, industrial products, and renewable energy sources, driving innovation, economic growth, and scientific advancement in SIDS.

5. Renewable Energy:

Renewable energy from marine resources, such as offshore wind, tidal energy, wave energy, and ocean thermal energy conversion (OTEC), presents opportunities for clean energy generation and energy security in SIDS. Marine renewable energy projects harness the power of ocean currents, waves, and tides to produce electricity, reduce dependency on fossil fuels, and mitigate greenhouse gas emissions, contributing to climate resilience and sustainability.

6. Desalination:

Desalination technologies provide a solution for addressing water scarcity and improving access to clean drinking water in SIDS. Sustainable desalination practices, such as reverse osmosis, solar desalination, and membrane distillation, reduce energy consumption, minimize environmental impacts, and enhance water security for coastal communities, supporting human well-being and sustainable development in SIDS.

7. Marine Tourism and Recreation:

Marine tourism and recreation activities, such as snorkeling, diving, sailing, and wildlife watching, are important drivers of the blue economy in SIDS. Sustainable tourism practices, such as marine ecotourism, responsible boating, and low-impact recreational activities, promote conservation awareness, support local economies, and generate revenue while safeguarding marine ecosystems and biodiversity.

8. Integrated Coastal Zone Management (ICZM):

Integrated Coastal Zone Management (ICZM) approaches promote the sustainable management of coastal resources and habitats in SIDS. ICZM frameworks, such as stakeholder engagement, land-use planning, ecosystem-based management, and adaptive governance, enhance resilience to climate change, reduce coastal risks, and support sustainable development in coastal areas.

In summary, harnessing marine resources sustainably is essential for promoting economic growth, ensuring food security, and conserving biodiversity in Small Island Developing States (SIDS). By adopting sustainable management practices, promoting innovation, and fostering multi-stakeholder collaboration, SIDS can unlock the economic, social, and environmental benefits of their marine resources while ensuring their long-term sustainability and resilience.

In conclusion, ocean conservation and sustainable marine resources management are essential for the long-term prosperity and resilience of Small Island

Chapter – 8

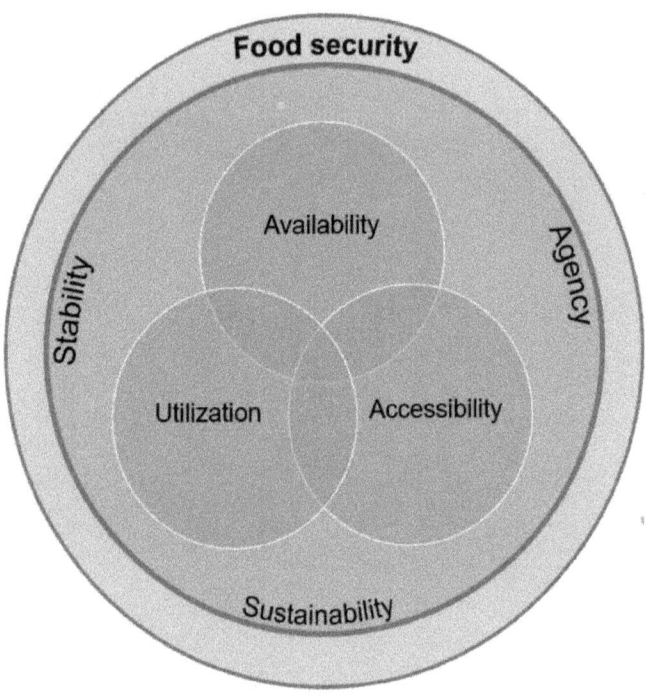

Sustainable Agriculture and Food Security

Small Island Developing States (SIDS) face unique challenges in agricultural production due to their limited land area, vulnerability to climate change, and dependence on imported food. This chapter explores the challenges in agricultural production, the promotion of agroecological practices, addressing food security concerns, and building resilience in agricultural systems.

8.1 Challenges in Agricultural Production

SIDS encounter several challenges in agricultural production that hinder food security and economic development:

- **Limited Arable Land:** SIDS have limited arable land available for agriculture due to small land size, rugged terrain, and competing land uses, restricting agricultural expansion and intensification.

- **Climate Variability:** SIDS are highly vulnerable to climate change impacts, including extreme weather events, droughts, floods, and sea-level rise, which disrupt agricultural production, damage crops, and degrade soil quality.

- **Water Scarcity:** SIDS face water scarcity and limited access to freshwater resources for irrigation, livestock watering, and domestic use, exacerbating agricultural challenges and compromising crop yields.

- **Soil Degradation:** Unsustainable land management practices, such as deforestation, soil erosion, and chemical-intensive agriculture, degrade soil fertility, reduce productivity, and threaten long-term agricultural sustainability.

- **Pest and Disease Pressure:** SIDS contend with pest and disease outbreaks that affect crop health and productivity, exacerbated by globalization, trade, and climate change, requiring integrated pest management (IPM) and biosecurity measures.

- **Dependence on Imports:** SIDS rely heavily on imported food to meet domestic consumption needs, exposing them to food price volatility, supply chain disruptions, and external shocks, compromising food security and self-sufficiency.

Addressing these challenges requires adopting sustainable agricultural practices that enhance productivity, resilience, and environmental sustainability.

Agriculture forms a critical sector in Small Island Developing States (SIDS), supporting food security, livelihoods, and economic development. However, SIDS face numerous challenges in agricultural production, stemming from their unique geographic, environmental, and socio-economic characteristics. This section examines the key challenges hindering agricultural production in SIDS and explores strategies to address them.

1. Limited Arable Land:
SIDS typically have limited land available for agriculture due to their small size, topographic constraints, and vulnerability to natural hazards such as hurricanes and floods. The scarcity of arable land restricts agricultural expansion and intensification, posing challenges for increasing food production and agricultural sustainability in SIDS.

2. Climate Change Impacts:
Climate change exacerbates agricultural challenges in SIDS, leading to unpredictable weather patterns, increased frequency and intensity of extreme events,

and rising temperatures. Heat stress, droughts, floods, saltwater intrusion, and pest outbreaks threaten crop yields, livestock productivity, and food security in SIDS, necessitating adaptive strategies and resilient farming practices.

3. Water Scarcity and Irrigation Challenges:

Water scarcity is a significant constraint on agricultural production in SIDS, where freshwater resources are limited and vulnerable to contamination and depletion. Inefficient irrigation practices, inadequate water storage facilities, and competing demands for water exacerbate water scarcity challenges, limiting agricultural productivity and hindering rural development in SIDS.

4. Soil Degradation and Erosion:

Soil degradation and erosion are pervasive problems in SIDS, resulting from deforestation, unsustainable land use practices, and extreme weather events. Soil erosion reduces soil fertility, degrades agricultural productivity, and exacerbates nutrient runoff and sedimentation in coastal waters, threatening ecosystems and marine biodiversity in SIDS.

5. Pest and Disease Management:

Pest and disease outbreaks pose significant threats to agricultural production in SIDS, affecting crops, livestock, and aquaculture systems. Invasive species, pests, and pathogens spread rapidly in SIDS due to global trade, climate change, and inadequate biosecurity measures, causing crop losses, economic losses, and food insecurity for rural communities.

6. Limited Access to Inputs and Technology:

Limited access to agricultural inputs, modern technology, and extension services constrains agricultural productivity and innovation in SIDS. High input costs, inadequate infrastructure, and lack of technical expertise hinder farmers' ability to adopt improved farming practices, mechanization, and technology solutions, limiting their resilience and competitiveness in global markets.

7. Market Access and Trade Barriers:

Market access and trade barriers present challenges for agricultural producers in SIDS, limiting their ability to compete in international markets and access value-added opportunities. Trade restrictions, tariffs, quotas, and non-tariff barriers hinder market integration, reduce export earnings, and constrain agricultural diversification and value chain development in SIDS.

8. Land Tenure and Property Rights:

Land tenure insecurity and inadequate property rights frameworks impede agricultural development and investment in SIDS. Unclear land tenure arrangements, overlapping land claims, and informal land tenure systems hinder land consolidation, investment in land improvements, and access to credit for smallholder farmers, limiting their ability to adopt sustainable farming practices and enhance productivity.

In summary, Small Island Developing States (SIDS) face multifaceted challenges in agricultural production, stemming from land constraints, climate change impacts, water scarcity, soil degradation, pest and disease pressures, limited access to inputs and technology, market access barriers, and land tenure issues. Addressing these challenges requires integrated approaches, policy interventions, and investments in resilient agriculture, sustainable land management, and rural development to enhance food security, livelihoods, and resilience in SIDS.

8.2 Promoting Agroecological Practices

Agroecological practices offer sustainable solutions to enhance agricultural productivity, conserve natural resources, and promote ecosystem resilience:

- **Agroforestry:** SIDS implement agroforestry systems that integrate trees, shrubs, and crops to diversify production, improve soil fertility, enhance biodiversity, and provide multiple ecosystem services, such as shade, windbreaks, and carbon sequestration.

- **Organic Farming:** SIDS promote organic farming methods that minimize the use of synthetic inputs, such as pesticides and fertilizers, reduce environmental pollution, protect soil health, and produce nutritious and chemical-free food.

- **Conservation Agriculture:** SIDS adopt conservation agriculture techniques, including minimum tillage, crop rotation, and cover cropping, to reduce soil disturbance, retain soil moisture, prevent erosion, and improve soil structure and fertility.

- **Agroecological Crop Management:** SIDS practice agroecological crop management techniques, such as intercropping, companion planting, and crop diversification, to enhance pest and disease resilience, optimize resource use, and increase farm productivity.

- **Sustainable Livestock Management:** SIDS promote sustainable livestock management practices, such as rotational grazing, silvopastoral systems, and organic feed production, to reduce environmental impacts, improve animal welfare, and enhance nutrient cycling.

By promoting agroecological practices, SIDS can build resilient and sustainable agricultural systems that enhance food security, support rural livelihoods, and conserve natural resources.

In response to the challenges faced by agriculture in Small Island Developing States (SIDS), promoting agroecological practices has emerged as a sustainable approach to enhance food security, resilience, and environmental sustainability. This section delves into the principles of agroecology and explores strategies for promoting its adoption in agricultural systems within SIDS.

1. Understanding Agroecology:

Agroecology is a holistic approach to agriculture that integrates ecological principles, traditional knowledge, and modern science to design and manage farming systems in harmony with nature. It emphasizes biodiversity, soil health, water conservation, and ecosystem services to enhance productivity, resilience, and sustainability in agricultural production.

2. Diversification of Cropping Systems:

Agroecological practices promote the diversification of cropping systems through intercropping, crop rotation, and polyculture, which enhance soil fertility, pest and disease resistance, and nutrient cycling. Diverse cropping systems mitigate the risks of crop failure, improve ecosystem resilience, and provide multiple benefits for farmers, such as increased yields, reduced input costs, and improved nutrition.

3. Soil Conservation and Restoration:

Agroecology prioritizes soil conservation and restoration measures, such as organic matter management, cover cropping, and agroforestry, to improve soil health, structure, and fertility. These practices enhance soil water retention, reduce erosion, and promote nutrient cycling, leading to higher yields, improved crop quality, and long-term sustainability of agricultural production in SIDS.

4. Water-Efficient Farming Techniques:

Agroecological practices include water-efficient farming techniques, such as rainwater harvesting, drip irrigation, and mulching, to optimize water use efficiency and enhance drought resilience in agricultural systems. By capturing and storing rainwater, reducing evaporation, and minimizing runoff, these techniques ensure reliable water supply for crops, livestock, and ecosystems in water-stressed SIDS.

5. Agrobiodiversity Conservation:

Agroecology promotes the conservation and utilization of agrobiodiversity, including traditional crop varieties, local livestock breeds, and indigenous agroforestry species, to enhance resilience and adaptation in agricultural systems. Preserving genetic diversity, conserving heirloom seeds, and promoting on-farm biodiversity contribute to ecosystem health, food security, and cultural heritage conservation in SIDS.

6. Integrated Pest Management (IPM):

Agroecological approaches emphasize Integrated Pest Management (IPM) strategies to control pests and diseases while minimizing reliance on synthetic pesticides and herbicides. IPM practices, such as biological control, crop rotation, and habitat manipulation, promote natural pest regulation, reduce chemical inputs, and protect beneficial insects, birds, and soil organisms in agroecosystems.

7. Farmer-Led Research and Knowledge Exchange:

Agroecology encourages farmer-led research, participatory learning, and knowledge exchange networks to co-create sustainable farming solutions and adapt practices to local contexts in SIDS. Farmer field schools, participatory research trials, and agroecology training programs empower farmers to experiment with innovative techniques, share experiences, and build collective capacity for agroecological innovation and adaptation.

8. Policy Support and Institutional Collaboration:

Promoting agroecological practices requires supportive policy frameworks, incentives, and institutional collaboration to mainstream sustainable agriculture in SIDS. Policy interventions, such as agroecology subsidies, extension services, and research funding, incentivize farmers to adopt environmentally friendly practices, while multi-stakeholder partnerships, involving government agencies, research institutions, civil society organizations, and farmers' associations, facilitate knowledge sharing, capacity building, and policy dialogue on agroecology.

In summary, promoting agroecological practices offers a holistic and sustainable approach to address the challenges of agriculture in Small Island Developing States (SIDS). By embracing agroecology principles, fostering innovation, and strengthening policy support, SIDS can enhance food security, resilience, and environmental sustainability in agricultural systems, while preserving natural resources and cultural heritage for future generations.

8.3 Addressing Food Security Concerns

Food security is a pressing concern for SIDS, given their vulnerability to external shocks and dependence on imported food:

- **Diversification of Food Sources:** SIDS promote the diversification of food sources, including traditional crops, indigenous food plants, drought-resistant varieties, and climate-resilient crops, to enhance dietary diversity, nutritional quality, and food self-sufficiency.

- **Strengthening Local Food Systems:** SIDS support local food systems, including small-scale farming, backyard gardening, community gardens, and farmers' markets, to reduce reliance on imported food, support local producers, and improve access to fresh and nutritious food.

- **Food Storage and Preservation:** SIDS invest in food storage and preservation facilities, such as cold storage units, drying facilities, and food processing centers, to reduce post-harvest losses, extend shelf life, and ensure food security during emergencies.

- **Climate-Resilient Agriculture:** SIDS promote climate-resilient agricultural practices, such as rainwater harvesting, drought-tolerant crops, and climate-smart irrigation, to adapt to changing climatic conditions, mitigate risks, and safeguard food production.

- **Enhancing Agricultural Extension Services:** SIDS strengthen agricultural extension services, farmer training programs, and knowledge-sharing networks to disseminate best practices, provide technical assistance, and build capacity among farmers, extension agents, and agricultural researchers.

By addressing food security concerns, SIDS can enhance the resilience of their food systems, reduce vulnerability to external shocks, and ensure access to safe, nutritious, and affordable food for all.

Food security remains a pressing challenge for Small Island Developing States (SIDS), where limited land availability, vulnerability to climate change, and dependence on imported food contribute to food insecurity and malnutrition. This section explores strategies to address food security concerns in SIDS through sustainable agriculture, improved nutrition, and enhanced resilience.

1. Enhancing Agricultural Productivity:

Increasing agricultural productivity is essential for enhancing food security in SIDS. Adopting sustainable farming practices, such as agroecology, conservation agriculture, and integrated crop-livestock systems, improves yields, reduces post-harvest losses, and enhances resilience to climate change, ensuring a stable food supply for local communities.

2. Diversifying Food Production:

Diversifying food production is crucial for reducing reliance on imported food and enhancing dietary diversity in SIDS. Promoting the cultivation of nutritious crops, indigenous varieties, and climate-resilient crops diversifies food sources, improves nutrition, and strengthens food security resilience against external shocks and price fluctuations.

3. Strengthening Food Value Chains:

Strengthening food value chains enhances market access, facilitates trade, and promotes local food production in SIDS. Investing in infrastructure, storage facilities, transportation networks, and market linkages improves the efficiency of food distribution, reduces food losses, and increases farmers' income, contributing to food security and rural development.

4. Improving Nutrition and Dietary Diversity:

Improving nutrition and dietary diversity is essential for addressing malnutrition and promoting public health in SIDS. Nutrition education, community gardens, and school feeding programs raise awareness of healthy eating habits, promote the consumption of diverse, nutrient-rich foods, and combat malnutrition, stunting, and micronutrient deficiencies among vulnerable populations.

5. Strengthening Social Safety Nets:

Strengthening social safety nets, such as food assistance programs, social welfare schemes, and disaster relief efforts, provides a crucial safety net for vulnerable populations during times of crisis in SIDS. Targeted interventions, such as cash transfers, food vouchers, and nutrition supplements, ensure access to food and basic necessities for marginalized groups, reducing hunger and poverty in SIDS.

6. Building Resilience to Climate Change:

Building resilience to climate change is essential for safeguarding food security in SIDS. Implementing climate-smart agriculture practices, such as drought-resistant crops, rainwater harvesting, and agroforestry, enhances agricultural resilience, reduces vulnerability to extreme weather events, and ensures the availability of food during periods of environmental stress.

7. Enhancing Governance and Policy Support:

Enhancing governance and policy support is critical for addressing food security concerns in SIDS. Developing national food security strategies, strengthening regulatory frameworks, and promoting multi-stakeholder collaboration facilitate coordinated action, resource mobilization, and policy coherence to address food security challenges and promote sustainable agriculture and rural development in SIDS.

8. Fostering Partnerships and International Cooperation:

Fostering partnerships and international cooperation is essential for addressing food security concerns in SIDS. Collaborating with international organizations, donor agencies, and development partners facilitates knowledge exchange, technology transfer, and financial support for food security initiatives, enhancing the resilience and sustainability of food systems in SIDS.

In summary, addressing food security concerns requires a multi-faceted approach that integrates sustainable agriculture, improved nutrition, and enhanced resilience in Small Island Developing States (SIDS). By promoting diversified food production, strengthening food value chains, and building resilience to climate change, SIDS can ensure access to nutritious food, reduce hunger, and promote sustainable development for present and future generations.

8.4 Building Resilience in Agricultural Systems

Building resilience in agricultural systems is essential for SIDS to adapt to climate change, mitigate risks, and ensure food security:

- **Climate-Resilient Crop Varieties:** SIDS develop and promote climate-resilient crop varieties, including drought-tolerant, heat-resistant, and pest-resistant varieties, through breeding programs, research partnerships, and seed banks.

- **Water Management Strategies:** SIDS implement water management strategies, such as rainwater harvesting, drip irrigation, and soil moisture conservation techniques, to optimize water use efficiency, mitigate drought impacts, and enhance crop resilience.

- **Disaster Preparedness and Response:** SIDS strengthen disaster preparedness and response mechanisms for agriculture, including early warning systems, emergency funds, crop insurance schemes, and post-disaster recovery plans, to minimize losses and support farmers during crises.

- **Soil Conservation and Restoration:** SIDS promote soil conservation and restoration measures, such as agroforestry, cover cropping, and soil rehabilitation techniques, to prevent soil erosion, improve soil health, and enhance agricultural productivity.

- **Community-Based Adaptation:** SIDS engage local communities in participatory adaptation planning, decision-making, and implementation of resilience-building initiatives, empowering farmers as agents of change and enhancing community resilience to climate change impacts.

By building resilience in agricultural systems, SIDS can strengthen food security, reduce vulnerability to climate risks, and promote sustainable livelihoods for rural communities.

Building resilience in agricultural systems is crucial for ensuring food security, sustaining livelihoods, and enhancing adaptation to climate change in Small Island Developing States (SIDS). This section explores strategies to strengthen the resilience of agricultural systems in SIDS, emphasizing climate-smart practices, risk management, and adaptive capacity building.

1. Climate-Smart Agriculture:

Climate-smart agriculture integrates climate resilience, sustainable productivity, and mitigation of greenhouse gas emissions into agricultural practices. Adopting climate-smart practices, such as agroforestry, conservation agriculture, and climate-resilient crop varieties, enhances the adaptive capacity of agricultural systems, improves yields, and reduces vulnerability to climate change impacts in SIDS.

2. Soil Conservation and Management:

Soil conservation and management practices are essential for maintaining soil fertility, moisture retention, and erosion control in agricultural systems. Implementing soil conservation measures, such as terracing, contour farming, and cover cropping, preserves soil health, enhances water infiltration, and mitigates erosion risks, ensuring the long-term sustainability of agriculture in SIDS.

3. Water-Efficient Farming Techniques:

Water-efficient farming techniques optimize water use efficiency and enhance drought resilience in agricultural systems. Investing in water-saving technologies, such as drip irrigation, rainwater harvesting, and soil moisture sensors, minimizes water wastage, conserves water resources, and sustains crop production during periods of water scarcity in SIDS.

4. Crop Diversification and Genetic Resources Conservation:

Crop diversification and conservation of genetic resources enhance the resilience and adaptability of agricultural systems to changing environmental conditions in SIDS. Promoting the cultivation of diverse crop varieties, traditional landraces, and climate-resilient crops diversifies food sources, buffers against crop failures, and preserves genetic diversity for future breeding efforts.

5. Livestock and Fisheries Management:

Sustainable management of livestock and fisheries resources is essential for building resilience in agricultural systems and supporting rural livelihoods in

SIDS. Adopting sustainable livestock management practices, such as rotational grazing, improved animal husbandry, and disease control measures, reduces pressure on natural resources and enhances resilience to climate-related risks. Similarly, implementing sustainable fisheries management measures, such as marine protected areas, seasonal closures, and responsible fishing practices, ensures the long-term viability of fisheries resources and supports food security in SIDS.

6. Agroecological Approaches:

Agroecological approaches promote the integration of ecological principles, traditional knowledge, and modern science to design resilient farming systems in SIDS. Adopting agroecological practices, such as agroforestry, intercropping, and integrated pest management, enhances biodiversity, soil health, and ecosystem services, improving the resilience and sustainability of agricultural production in SIDS.

7. Disaster Risk Reduction and Preparedness:

Disaster risk reduction and preparedness measures are essential for mitigating the impacts of natural hazards on agricultural systems in SIDS. Developing early warning systems, emergency response plans, and risk transfer mechanisms, such as crop insurance and social safety nets, enhances resilience, reduces losses, and facilitates recovery from climate-related disasters in SIDS.

8. Capacity Building and Knowledge Sharing:

Capacity building and knowledge sharing initiatives empower farmers, extension workers, and agricultural stakeholders to adopt climate-resilient practices and enhance adaptive capacity in SIDS. Providing training, technical assistance, and information sharing platforms fosters innovation, builds resilience, and promotes sustainable agriculture and rural development in SIDS.

In summary, building resilience in agricultural systems is essential for enhancing food security, sustaining livelihoods, and promoting sustainable development in Small Island Developing States (SIDS). By adopting climate-smart practices, conserving genetic resources, and investing in disaster risk reduction measures, SIDS can strengthen the resilience of agricultural systems and enhance their capacity to adapt to climate change impacts and other challenges.

In conclusion, sustainable agriculture and food security are critical components of the development agenda for Small Island Developing States. By promoting agroecological practices, addressing food security concerns, and building resilience in agricultural systems, SIDS can enhance food security, reduce vulnerability, and achieve sustainable development goals for their citizens.

Chapter – 9

Drinking water and human well-being

Ecosystems

Water security

Economic activities and development

Water related hazards and climate change

Access to Clean Water and Sanitation

Access to clean water and sanitation is essential for the health, well-being, and sustainable development of Small Island Developing States (SIDS). This chapter examines the challenges of water scarcity, strategies for water management, innovative solutions for clean water access, and the importance of sanitation infrastructure for public health.

9.1 Water Scarcity Issues

Water scarcity is a significant challenge for many SIDS due to their limited freshwater resources, population growth, and climate change impacts:

- **Limited Freshwater Resources:** SIDS often face constraints in freshwater availability due to small land size, low rainfall, and limited groundwater reserves, leading to water scarcity and competition for water resources.

- **Population Growth:** Rapid population growth and urbanization in SIDS strain water supply systems, increase water demand for domestic, industrial, and agricultural uses, and exacerbate water stress in densely populated areas.

- **Climate Change Impacts:** Climate change exacerbates water scarcity in SIDS through changing precipitation patterns, increased evaporation, and saltwater intrusion into freshwater sources, compromising water quality and availability.

Addressing water scarcity requires sustainable water management practices and investments in water infrastructure and conservation measures.

Water scarcity poses a significant challenge for Small Island Developing States (SIDS), where limited freshwater resources, growing demand for water, and vulnerability to climate change exacerbate water stress and threaten water security. This section examines the water scarcity issues facing SIDS, including the drivers, impacts, and implications for sustainable development.

1. Limited Freshwater Resources:

SIDS typically have limited freshwater resources due to their small size, low rainfall, and geological constraints. Many SIDS rely on rainfall-dependent surface water sources, such as rivers, lakes, and reservoirs, for domestic, agricultural, and industrial water supply, making them vulnerable to fluctuations in precipitation patterns and drought events.

2. Growing Water Demand:

Growing population, urbanization, tourism development, and industrialization increase water demand in SIDS, straining already limited water resources and exacerbating water scarcity issues. Rising water demand for domestic consumption, irrigation, tourism facilities, and industrial activities intensifies competition for water, leading to conflicts, water shortages, and environmental degradation in SIDS.

3. Climate Change Impacts:

Climate change exacerbates water scarcity issues in SIDS, altering precipitation patterns, increasing evaporation rates, and intensifying extreme weather events, such as droughts and floods. Rising temperatures, changing rainfall patterns, and sea-level rise exacerbate water stress, salinization of freshwater sources, and coastal inundation, threatening water availability, quality, and reliability in SIDS.

4. Water Pollution and Contamination:

Water pollution and contamination degrade freshwater quality and exacerbate water scarcity issues in SIDS. Pollution from agricultural runoff, untreated sewage, solid waste, and industrial discharge contaminates surface water sources, groundwater aquifers, and coastal ecosystems, jeopardizing public health, ecosystem integrity, and water security in SIDS.

5. Inadequate Water Infrastructure:

Inadequate water infrastructure and sanitation facilities impede access to clean water and exacerbate water scarcity issues in SIDS. Limited piped water networks, inadequate storage facilities, and unreliable water supply systems contribute to water shortages, waterborne diseases, and poor hygiene practices, particularly in rural and peri-urban areas of SIDS.

6. Water Governance Challenges:

Water governance challenges, such as fragmented institutional arrangements, weak regulatory frameworks, and lack of capacity, hinder effective water management and exacerbate water scarcity issues in SIDS. Inadequate water governance undermines coordination, planning, and investment in water infrastructure, management, and conservation efforts, hampering progress towards achieving water security and sustainable development goals in SIDS.

7. Socio-Economic Impacts:

Water scarcity has significant socio-economic impacts on communities, livelihoods, and ecosystems in SIDS. Limited access to clean water affects public health, sanitation, and hygiene practices, leading to waterborne diseases, malnutrition, and poverty. Water shortages also disrupt agricultural production, industrial activities, and tourism operations, compromising economic growth, food security, and resilience in SIDS.

8. Climate Resilience and Adaptation Strategies:

Building climate resilience and adaptation strategies is essential for addressing water scarcity issues in SIDS. Implementing water conservation measures, such as rainwater harvesting, water recycling, and efficient irrigation practices, reduces water demand, enhances water efficiency, and improves drought resilience in SIDS. Integrating climate resilience into water infrastructure planning, management, and investment decisions also enhances adaptive capacity and ensures sustainable water management in SIDS.

In summary, water scarcity issues pose significant challenges for Small Island Developing States (SIDS), threatening water security, public health, and socio-economic development. By addressing the drivers of water scarcity, improving water governance, and implementing climate-resilient water management strategies, SIDS can enhance water security, build resilience, and promote sustainable development for present and future generations.

9.2 Water Management Strategies

Water management is paramount for Small Island Developing States (SIDS) to address water scarcity, ensure water security, and promote sustainable development. This section explores various water management strategies adopted by SIDS to efficiently utilize and conserve their limited freshwater resources.

1. Integrated Water Resource Management (IWRM):

Integrated Water Resource Management (IWRM) approaches promote the coordinated and sustainable management of water resources in SIDS. IWRM emphasizes stakeholder participation, multi-sectoral collaboration, and ecosystem-based approaches to water management, ensuring equitable access to water, protecting water quality, and enhancing resilience to climate change impacts.

2. Water Conservation and Demand Management:

Water conservation and demand management measures aim to reduce water consumption, minimize water losses, and improve water use efficiency in SIDS. Implementing water-saving technologies, such as low-flow fixtures, water-efficient appliances, and drip irrigation systems, reduces water demand, conserves water resources, and supports sustainable water management practices in SIDS.

3. Rainwater Harvesting and Storage:

Rainwater harvesting and storage systems capture and store rainwater for domestic, agricultural, and industrial use in SIDS. Installing rainwater harvesting infrastructure, such as rooftop catchment systems, cisterns, and reservoirs, increases water availability, supplements water supply during dry seasons, and enhances resilience to droughts and water scarcity in SIDS.

4. Water Recycling and Reuse:

Water recycling and reuse practices treat wastewater and greywater for non-potable purposes, such as irrigation, landscaping, and industrial processes, in SIDS. Implementing water reuse systems, such as decentralized wastewater treatment plants, water recycling schemes, and constructed wetlands, conserves freshwater resources, reduces pollution, and promotes sustainable water management practices in SIDS.

5. Desalination and Water Desalination Technologies:

Desalination technologies convert seawater or brackish water into freshwater through processes such as reverse osmosis, distillation, and electrodialysis in SIDS. Deploying desalination plants and decentralized desalination systems provides a reliable source of freshwater, enhances water security, and mitigates water scarcity risks in coastal SIDS facing freshwater shortages.

6. Groundwater Management and Aquifer Recharge:

Groundwater management and aquifer recharge initiatives sustainably manage groundwater resources and replenish depleted aquifers in SIDS. Implementing groundwater monitoring systems, regulating groundwater abstraction, and promoting artificial recharge techniques, such as infiltration basins and injection wells, sustain groundwater levels, prevent saltwater intrusion, and safeguard water quality in SIDS.

7. Ecosystem-based Approaches to Water Management:

Ecosystem-based approaches to water management harness the natural functions of ecosystems to enhance water quality, regulate water flow, and provide water-related services in SIDS. Protecting and restoring watersheds, wetlands, and mangrove forests preserve water catchment areas, mitigate floods, reduce erosion, and improve water filtration, contributing to sustainable water management and biodiversity conservation in SIDS.

8. Capacity Building and Institutional Strengthening:

Capacity building and institutional strengthening initiatives enhance the technical capacity, governance structures, and regulatory frameworks for water management in SIDS. Providing training, technical assistance, and institutional support to water authorities, local governments, and community-based organizations fosters effective water governance, promotes stakeholder engagement, and facilitates sustainable water management practices in SIDS.

In summary, adopting integrated and sustainable water management strategies is essential for addressing water scarcity, ensuring water security, and promoting sustainable development in Small Island Developing States (SIDS). By implementing water conservation measures, investing in water infrastructure, and enhancing institutional capacity, SIDS can effectively manage their freshwater resources, mitigate water scarcity risks, and build resilience to climate change impacts.

9.3 Innovative Solutions for Clean Water Access

Innovative solutions play a crucial role in expanding access to clean water in SIDS:

- **Solar-Powered Water Systems:** SIDS deploy solar-powered water pumping and purification systems to provide off-grid communities with reliable access to clean water, utilizing solar energy to power water pumps, filtration units, and disinfection technologies.

- **Mobile Water Treatment Units:** SIDS utilize mobile water treatment units equipped with filtration, disinfection, and monitoring equipment to respond to emergencies, natural disasters, and humanitarian crises, providing safe drinking water to affected populations.

- **Water ATM Machines:** SIDS install water ATM machines in urban and peri-urban areas to dispense clean drinking water on a pay-per-use basis, improving access to safe water for low-income households and informal settlements.

- **Community-Led Water Projects:** SIDS support community-led water projects, such as rainwater harvesting systems, communal wells, and water kiosks, empowering local communities to manage their water resources, address water needs, and promote social equity and inclusion.

By embracing innovative solutions, SIDS can overcome barriers to clean water access, expand coverage, and improve water quality for all citizens.

Access to clean water is fundamental for human health, sanitation, and sustainable development in Small Island Developing States (SIDS). This section explores innovative solutions and technologies that are addressing the challenge of providing clean water access in SIDS, overcoming constraints such as limited freshwater resources, water scarcity, and contamination.

1. Solar-Powered Desalination Plants:

Solar-powered desalination plants harness solar energy to convert seawater or brackish water into freshwater through desalination processes. Deploying solar desalination technologies provides a sustainable and energy-efficient solution for producing clean water in coastal SIDS, where freshwater resources are scarce, and energy availability is limited.

2. Mobile Water Treatment Units:

Mobile water treatment units are compact, portable systems equipped with filtration, disinfection, and purification technologies that can be deployed rapidly to provide clean water in emergency situations, remote areas, and underserved communities in SIDS. Mobile units offer flexibility, scalability, and cost-effectiveness for delivering safe drinking water to populations facing water scarcity and contamination risks.

3. Fog Harvesting Technology:

Fog harvesting technology captures moisture from fog-laden air using specially designed mesh nets or collectors, condensing it into liquid water for drinking, irrigation, and other uses in arid and semi-arid regions of SIDS. Fog harvesting systems offer a nature-based solution for supplementing water supply, particularly in mountainous and coastal areas where fog frequency is high.

4. Nanotechnology-Based Water Filters:

Nanotechnology-based water filters utilize nanomaterials, such as carbon nanotubes, graphene, and nanoparticles, to remove contaminants, pathogens, and pollutants from water at the molecular level. Nanofiltration and membrane technologies offer highly efficient and selective filtration capabilities, enabling the production of clean and safe drinking water from diverse water sources, including groundwater, surface water, and rainwater, in SIDS.

5. Atmospheric Water Generators (AWGs):

Atmospheric water generators extract moisture from the air through condensation processes, producing potable water without relying on traditional water sources in SIDS. AWGs utilize refrigeration or desiccant technologies to dehumidify air and collect condensed water vapor, providing a decentralized and off-grid solution for clean water access in remote and water-stressed areas of SIDS.

6. Bioremediation and Phytofiltration Systems:

Bioremediation and phytofiltration systems employ natural processes and living organisms, such as microorganisms, plants, and algae, to remove contaminants and pollutants from water bodies, groundwater, and wastewater effluents in SIDS.

Constructed wetlands, biofilters, and phytoremediation techniques offer cost-effective and environmentally friendly solutions for treating contaminated water and improving water quality in SIDS.

7. Community-Led Water Management Initiatives:

Community-led water management initiatives empower local communities to take ownership of water resources, develop water governance structures, and implement sustainable water management practices in SIDS. Participatory approaches, such as community-based water monitoring, water user associations, and decentralized water supply systems, promote social equity, resilience, and sustainability in water management and service delivery in SIDS.

8. Digital Water Technologies and Smart Water Systems:

Digital water technologies and smart water systems utilize sensors, data analytics, and real-time monitoring platforms to optimize water distribution, detect leaks, and manage water resources efficiently in SIDS. Deploying digital water solutions, such as smart meters, remote sensors, and cloud-based management systems, enhances water infrastructure resilience, reduces nonrevenue water losses, and improves water service delivery in SIDS.

In summary, innovative solutions for clean water access offer promising opportunities to address water scarcity, contamination, and access challenges in Small Island Developing States (SIDS). By embracing technology, nature-based solutions, and community engagement, SIDS can overcome water-related constraints, improve water quality, and ensure equitable access to clean and safe drinking water for all residents.

9.4 Sanitation Infrastructure and Public Health

Sanitation infrastructure plays a critical role in safeguarding public health and promoting sustainable development in Small Island Developing States (SIDS). This section examines the importance of sanitation infrastructure, the challenges faced by SIDS, and innovative approaches to improve sanitation and public health outcomes.

1. Importance of Sanitation Infrastructure:

Sanitation infrastructure, including toilets, sewage systems, and wastewater treatment facilities, is essential for preventing waterborne diseases, protecting environmental health, and ensuring the well-being of communities in SIDS. Access to safe sanitation facilities reduces the risk of water contamination, improves hygiene practices, and enhances public health outcomes, particularly among vulnerable populations.

2. Challenges in Sanitation Infrastructure:

SIDS face various challenges in sanitation infrastructure, including limited access to improved sanitation facilities, inadequate sewage systems, and poor wastewater management practices. Rapid population growth, urbanization, and tourism development strain existing sanitation infrastructure, leading to inadequate sanitation coverage, pollution of water bodies, and risks to public health in SIDS.

3. Innovative Sanitation Technologies:

Innovative sanitation technologies offer sustainable solutions to improve sanitation infrastructure and address public health challenges in SIDS. Eco-friendly toilets, composting toilets, and decentralized sanitation systems provide alternative sanitation options for areas with limited access to centralized sewage networks. Additionally, resource recovery technologies, such as biogas digesters and nutrient recovery systems, enable the reuse of wastewater and organic waste for energy generation and agricultural purposes in SIDS.

4. Decentralized Wastewater Treatment:

Decentralized wastewater treatment systems, such as constructed wetlands, decentralized sewage treatment plants, and biofiltration systems, offer decentralized solutions for treating wastewater and reducing pollution in SIDS. Implementing decentralized treatment options improves sanitation coverage, protects water quality, and enhances public health outcomes, particularly in peri-urban and rural areas with limited access to centralized sewage infrastructure.

5. Integrated Water and Sanitation Management:

Integrated water and sanitation management approaches promote the coordinated management of water resources and sanitation infrastructure to improve public health outcomes in SIDS. Integrating water supply, sanitation, and hygiene interventions enhances synergies, maximizes resource efficiency, and promotes sustainable development in SIDS, ensuring access to clean water and sanitation for all residents.

6. Behavior Change Communication and Hygiene Promotion:

Behavior change communication and hygiene promotion campaigns raise awareness of the importance of sanitation, promote good hygiene practices, and empower communities to adopt safe sanitation behaviors in SIDS. Educational programs, community-led initiatives, and social mobilization efforts encourage handwashing, toilet use, and safe sanitation practices, reducing the risk of waterborne diseases and improving public health outcomes in SIDS.

7. Policy Support and Institutional Capacity Building:

Policy support and institutional capacity building are essential for strengthening sanitation infrastructure and improving public health outcomes in SIDS. Developing national sanitation strategies, strengthening regulatory frameworks, and investing in sanitation infrastructure prioritize sanitation investments, mobilize resources, and promote multi-stakeholder collaboration to address sanitation challenges and achieve sustainable development goals in SIDS.

8. Partnerships and International Cooperation:

Partnerships and international cooperation play a crucial role in supporting sanitation infrastructure development and promoting public health outcomes in SIDS. Collaborating with international organizations, donor agencies, and development partners facilitates knowledge exchange, technology transfer, and financial support for sanitation projects, enhancing the resilience and sustainability of sanitation infrastructure in SIDS.

In summary, sanitation infrastructure is essential for protecting public health, preserving environmental quality, and promoting sustainable development in Small Island Developing States (SIDS). By investing in innovative technologies, promoting behavior change, and strengthening policy support, SIDS can improve sanitation coverage, reduce waterborne diseases, and ensure access to safe sanitation for all residents, contributing to healthier and more resilient communities.

In conclusion, access to clean water and sanitation is fundamental for sustainable development in Small Island Developing States. By addressing water scarcity, implementing effective water management strategies, embracing innovative solutions, and improving sanitation infrastructure, SIDS can achieve water security, protect public health, and advance towards a more sustainable future.

Chapter – 10

Cumulative and cascading impacts of recent compound events in the Maldives Islands

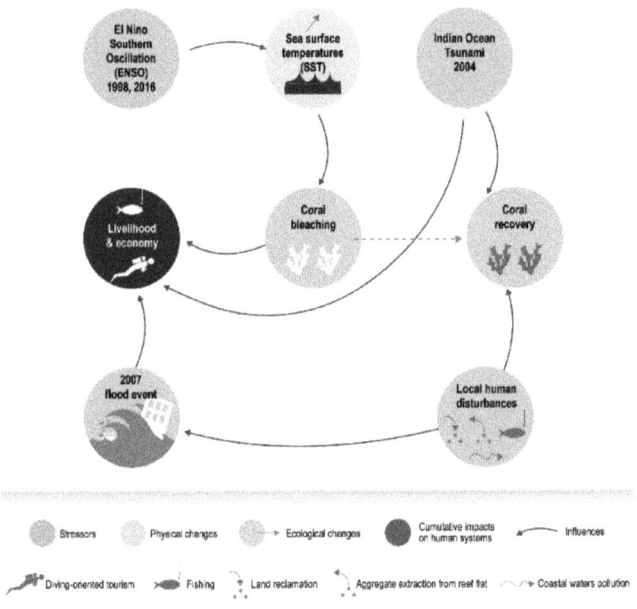

Governance, Policy, and Partnerships

Effective governance, robust policy frameworks, and meaningful partnerships are essential for driving sustainable development in Small Island Developing States (SIDS). This chapter delves into the importance of strengthening institutional capacity, crafting policy frameworks for sustainable development, engaging civil society and communities, and fostering international cooperation and partnerships.

10.1 Strengthening Institutional Capacity

Strengthening institutional capacity is crucial for Small Island Developing States (SIDS) to effectively implement sustainable development initiatives, address complex challenges, and achieve their development goals. This section examines the importance of institutional capacity, strategies for capacity building, and the role of institutions in promoting sustainable development in SIDS.

1. Importance of Institutional Capacity:

Institutional capacity refers to the ability of organizations, governments, and stakeholders to plan, implement, and monitor sustainable development initiatives effectively. Strong institutional capacity is essential for formulating policies, mobilizing resources, coordinating actions, and delivering services that promote economic, social, and environmental sustainability in SIDS.

2. Building Institutional Resilience:

Building institutional resilience involves enhancing the capacity of institutions to anticipate, adapt to, and recover from internal and external shocks and stresses. Strengthening governance structures, improving decision-making processes, and fostering organizational learning enable institutions to respond effectively to emerging challenges, such as climate change, natural disasters, and economic crises, in SIDS.

3. Enhancing Policy Formulation and Implementation:

Enhancing policy formulation and implementation capacity is critical for translating sustainable development goals into actionable policies and programs in SIDS. Developing evidence-based policies, mainstreaming sustainability principles, and promoting stakeholder participation in decision-making processes enhance policy coherence, effectiveness, and accountability in SIDS.

4. Strengthening Regulatory Frameworks:

Strengthening regulatory frameworks involves establishing and enforcing laws, regulations, and standards to promote sustainable development and protect environmental and social interests in SIDS. Implementing robust regulatory mechanisms, enhancing enforcement capacity, and promoting compliance with environmental, social, and economic regulations foster good governance, transparency, and accountability in SIDS.

5. Promoting Multi-Stakeholder Collaboration:

Promoting multi-stakeholder collaboration involves engaging diverse actors, including governments, civil society organizations, private sector entities, and local communities, in sustainable development efforts in SIDS. Facilitating dialogue, building partnerships, and fostering collaboration among stakeholders enhance collective action, leverage resources, and promote inclusive decision-making processes in SIDS.

6. Investing in Human Resources Development:

Investing in human resources development involves building the skills, knowledge, and expertise of individuals and organizations to effectively address sustainable development challenges in SIDS. Providing training, capacity building programs, and professional development opportunities for government officials, civil servants, and other stakeholders enhances institutional capacity, fosters innovation, and promotes adaptive management approaches in SIDS.

7. Harnessing Technology and Innovation:

Harnessing technology and innovation enables institutions to leverage digital tools, data analytics, and innovative solutions to address sustainable development challenges in SIDS. Embracing digital transformation, promoting open data initiatives, and fostering technological innovation enhance institutional efficiency, improve service delivery, and promote evidence-based decision-making in SIDS.

8. Promoting Knowledge Management and Learning:

Promoting knowledge management and learning involves sharing best practices, lessons learned, and experiences to inform policy-making, improve program design, and enhance institutional effectiveness in SIDS.

Establishing knowledge sharing platforms, conducting evaluations, and fostering communities of practice facilitate organizational learning, innovation, and continuous improvement in SIDS.

In summary, strengthening institutional capacity is essential for promoting sustainable development, enhancing resilience, and achieving development goals in Small Island Developing States (SIDS). By investing in institutional capacity building, promoting good governance, and fostering multi-stakeholder collaboration, SIDS can build resilient institutions, empower stakeholders, and advance sustainable development for present and future generations.

10.2 Policy Frameworks for Sustainable Development

Developing and implementing comprehensive policy frameworks are essential for guiding sustainable development efforts in SIDS:

- **National Development Plans:** SIDS formulate national development plans, strategies, and policies that integrate social, economic, and environmental considerations, set clear priorities and targets, and provide a roadmap for achieving sustainable development goals.

- **Climate Change Adaptation and Mitigation Plans:** SIDS develop climate change adaptation and mitigation plans that identify vulnerabilities, assess risks, and prioritize actions to build resilience, reduce greenhouse gas emissions, and adapt to changing climatic conditions.

- **Environmental Regulations:** SIDS enact and enforce environmental regulations, standards, and laws to protect natural resources, conserve biodiversity, and mitigate pollution, ensuring compliance with international agreements and conventions.

- **Sustainable Tourism Policies:** SIDS establish sustainable tourism policies and regulations that promote responsible tourism practices, protect cultural and natural heritage, and maximize economic benefits while minimizing negative environmental and social impacts.

By adopting coherent and integrated policy frameworks, SIDS can create an enabling environment for sustainable development, mobilize resources, and foster stakeholder participation and ownership.

Policy frameworks play a central role in guiding the sustainable development agenda and promoting holistic approaches to addressing the complex challenges faced by Small Island Developing States (SIDS). This section delves into the importance of policy frameworks, key components of effective policy development, and examples of policy initiatives in SIDS aimed at achieving sustainable development goals.

1. Importance of Policy Frameworks:

Policy frameworks provide a strategic roadmap for integrating economic, social, and environmental considerations into decision-making processes and promoting sustainable development in SIDS. Comprehensive policy frameworks establish priorities, set targets, allocate resources, and coordinate actions across sectors to address interconnected challenges, such as climate change, biodiversity loss, and poverty alleviation, in SIDS.

2. Integrated Policy Approaches:

Integrated policy approaches adopt a cross-cutting and holistic perspective to address interconnected challenges and promote synergies among economic, social, and environmental objectives in SIDS. Implementing integrated policy frameworks, such as

National Sustainable Development Strategies (NSDS) or Green Growth Plans, mainstreams sustainability principles into sectoral policies, fosters coordination among government agencies, and enhances coherence in decision-making processes in SIDS.

3. Mainstreaming Sustainable Development Goals (SDGs):

Mainstreaming Sustainable Development Goals (SDGs) involves aligning national development priorities, policies, and programs with the global SDG agenda to advance sustainable development in SIDS. Integrating SDGs into national policy frameworks, development plans, and budgetary processes enhances policy coherence, mobilizes resources, and accelerates progress towards achieving the 2030 Agenda in SIDS.

4. Climate Change Adaptation and Mitigation Policies:

Climate change adaptation and mitigation policies aim to enhance resilience, reduce vulnerability, and mitigate greenhouse gas emissions in response to climate change impacts in SIDS. Developing climate change adaptation plans, establishing climate resilience funds, and implementing renewable energy targets promote climate-resilient development pathways, reduce carbon footprints, and enhance climate change resilience in SIDS.

5. Biodiversity Conservation and Ecosystem Management Strategies:

Biodiversity conservation and ecosystem management strategies promote the sustainable use and conservation of natural resources, biodiversity, and ecosystems in SIDS. Developing protected area networks, implementing ecosystem-based approaches, and integrating biodiversity considerations into land-use planning and management enhance ecosystem resilience, safeguard ecosystem services, and preserve cultural and biological diversity in SIDS.

6. Sustainable Energy Policies:

Sustainable energy policies aim to promote the transition towards clean, renewable energy sources and improve energy access, efficiency, and affordability in SIDS. Implementing renewable energy targets, incentivizing investment in clean energy technologies, and promoting energy efficiency measures reduce dependence on fossil fuels, enhance energy security, and mitigate climate change impacts in SIDS.

7. Blue Economy Strategies:

Blue economy strategies harness the potential of marine and coastal resources to promote sustainable economic development, environmental conservation, and social well-being in SIDS. Developing blue economy policies, fostering sustainable fisheries management, and promoting marine conservation initiatives maximize economic benefits while minimizing negative environmental impacts, enhancing resilience, and promoting inclusive and equitable growth in SIDS.

8. Governance Reforms and Institutional Strengthening:

Governance reforms and institutional strengthening initiatives aim to enhance policy coherence, effectiveness, and accountability in promoting sustainable development in SIDS. Strengthening governance structures, improving regulatory frameworks, and enhancing stakeholder engagement promote transparency, accountability, and inclusive decision-making processes, fostering trust, legitimacy, and effectiveness of policy interventions in SIDS.

In summary, policy frameworks are essential for guiding the sustainable development agenda, promoting integrated approaches, and addressing the interconnected challenges faced by Small Island

Developing States (SIDS). By adopting holistic and inclusive policy approaches, mainstreaming sustainable development goals, and strengthening governance structures, SIDS can accelerate progress towards achieving sustainable development outcomes and building resilient and prosperous societies for present and future generations.

10.3 Role of Civil Society and Community Engagement

Civil society and community engagement play a vital role in promoting sustainable development, fostering social cohesion, and empowering local communities in Small Island Developing States (SIDS). This section explores the significance of civil society and community engagement, their contributions to sustainable development, and strategies for enhancing their involvement in decision-making processes.

1. Importance of Civil Society and Community Engagement:

Civil society organizations (CSOs) and community groups serve as key stakeholders in promoting sustainable development and advocating for the rights and interests of marginalized groups in SIDS. Their active participation in decision-making processes, policy formulation, and implementation enhances transparency, accountability, and inclusivity in governance, fostering democratic governance and social justice in SIDS.

2. Advocacy and Policy Influence:

Civil society organizations play a crucial role in advocating for policy reforms, influencing decision-making processes, and holding governments and other stakeholders accountable for their commitments to sustainable development in SIDS. Through research, analysis, and public awareness campaigns, CSOs raise awareness of pressing issues, mobilize public support, and advocate for policy changes that address social, economic, and environmental challenges in SIDS.

3. Community Empowerment and Capacity Building:

Community engagement initiatives empower local communities to participate in decision-making processes, identify their needs, and take collective action to address development challenges in SIDS. Facilitating community-led development projects, providing training and capacity-building programs, and promoting participatory approaches enhance community resilience, social capital, and ownership of development processes in SIDS.

4. Knowledge Sharing and Information Dissemination:

Civil society organizations serve as platforms for knowledge sharing, information dissemination, and awareness-raising on sustainable development issues in SIDS. Through workshops, forums, and outreach activities, CSOs provide communities with access to information, tools, and resources to make informed decisions, build awareness of their rights, and mobilize collective action towards achieving sustainable development goals in SIDS.

5. Monitoring and Accountability Mechanisms:

Civil society organizations play a critical role in monitoring progress towards sustainable development goals, tracking government commitments, and holding stakeholders accountable for their actions in SIDS. Through independent monitoring, data collection, and reporting mechanisms, CSOs provide feedback on policy implementation, highlight gaps and challenges, and advocate for policy reforms to address emerging issues and ensure transparency and accountability in SIDS.

6. Social Innovation and Grassroots Initiatives:

Civil society organizations drive social innovation and grassroots initiatives that address local needs, promote community resilience, and catalyze sustainable development in SIDS. Supporting community-led projects, fostering social entrepreneurship, and nurturing grassroots movements empower marginalized groups, promote bottom-up development approaches, and foster innovation and creativity in addressing sustainable development challenges in SIDS.

7. Strengthening Partnerships and Collaboration:

Civil society organizations strengthen partnerships and collaboration among stakeholders, including governments, private sector entities, and international organizations, to advance sustainable development agendas in SIDS. Engaging in multi-stakeholder dialogues, forging strategic alliances, and leveraging resources and expertise from diverse sectors enhance collective action, promote shared responsibility, and catalyze transformative change towards sustainable development in SIDS.

8. Inclusive Decision-Making Processes:

Promoting inclusive decision-making processes involves ensuring meaningful participation of civil society organizations and marginalized groups in policy formulation, implementation, and evaluation processes in SIDS. Fostering dialogue, building trust, and respecting diversity and indigenous knowledge systems enhance inclusivity, legitimacy, and effectiveness of decision-making processes, leading to more equitable and sustainable outcomes in SIDS.

In summary, civil society and community engagement are essential for promoting sustainable development, fostering democratic governance, and empowering local communities in Small Island Developing States (SIDS). By strengthening partnerships, promoting inclusive decision-making processes, and empowering communities to take ownership of development initiatives, SIDS can harness the collective efforts of civil society and local communities to achieve sustainable development goals and build resilient and inclusive societies for present and future generations.

10.4 International Cooperation and Partnerships

International cooperation and partnerships are essential for supporting sustainable development efforts in SIDS:

- **Official Development Assistance (ODA):** SIDS receive ODA, grants, concessional loans, and technical assistance from bilateral and multilateral donors, development agencies, and international financial institutions to finance sustainable development projects and programs.

- **South-South Cooperation:** SIDS engage in South-South cooperation initiatives with other developing countries to exchange knowledge, share best practices, and collaborate on capacity-building, technology transfer, and development projects in areas such as climate change, renewable energy, and agriculture.

- **Global Partnerships:** SIDS participate in global partnerships, alliances, and initiatives, such as the Alliance of Small Island States (AOSIS), the Small Island Developing States Accelerated Modalities of Action (SAMOA) Pathway, and the Sustainable Development Goals (SDGs), to advocate for their interests, mobilize support, and influence international agendas.

By leveraging international cooperation and partnerships, SIDS can access resources, expertise, and technology, leverage collective action, and address common challenges and opportunities in sustainable development.

International cooperation and partnerships are indispensable for addressing the complex challenges faced by Small Island Developing States (SIDS) and advancing sustainable development agendas. This section examines the importance of international cooperation, key areas of collaboration, and examples of successful partnerships that support sustainable development in SIDS.

1. Importance of International Cooperation:

International cooperation facilitates the exchange of knowledge, resources, and expertise among countries, international organizations, and stakeholders, enabling SIDS to address common challenges and achieve sustainable development goals. By pooling resources, sharing best practices, and coordinating efforts, international cooperation strengthens resilience, promotes innovation, and fosters solidarity among nations facing similar development challenges.

2. Climate Finance and Adaptation Funding:

International cooperation plays a crucial role in mobilizing climate finance and adaptation funding to support SIDS in addressing the impacts of climate change and building resilience. Initiatives such as the Green Climate Fund, the Adaptation Fund, and bilateral aid programs provide financial assistance for climate change adaptation projects, renewable energy development, and disaster risk reduction initiatives in SIDS.

3. Technical Assistance and Capacity Building:

International cooperation facilitates the provision of technical assistance and capacity building support to enhance the resilience and sustainability of SIDS. Through capacity building programs, knowledge sharing initiatives, and technology transfer, international partners assist SIDS in strengthening institutional capacity, developing human resources, and implementing sustainable development initiatives in areas such as renewable energy, water management, and biodiversity conservation.

4. Multilateral Agreements and Treaties:

Multilateral agreements and treaties serve as frameworks for international cooperation and collaboration on global challenges such as climate change, biodiversity conservation, and sustainable development. Treaties such as the Paris Agreement, the Convention on Biological Diversity, and the Sustainable Development Goals (SDGs) provide platforms for SIDS to engage with the international community, exchange best practices, and advocate for their interests on the global stage.

5. South-South Cooperation:

South-South cooperation promotes collaboration among developing countries, including SIDS, to share knowledge, experiences, and resources for mutual development benefit. Through initiatives such as technical exchanges, capacity-building programs, and triangular cooperation arrangements, SIDS leverage the expertise and resources of other developing countries to address common challenges, promote inclusive development, and foster solidarity within the Global South.

6. Public-Private Partnerships (PPPs):

Public-private partnerships (PPPs) facilitate collaboration between governments, private sector entities, and civil society organizations to mobilize resources, innovate solutions, and implement sustainable development projects in SIDS. PPPs leverage the expertise, technology, and investment capital of the private sector to support infrastructure development, renewable energy projects, and sustainable tourism initiatives, fostering economic growth and resilience in SIDS.

7. Regional and Sub-Regional Initiatives:

Regional and sub-regional initiatives promote cooperation and integration among neighboring SIDS to address shared challenges and pursue common development goals. Regional organizations such as the

Caribbean Community (CARICOM), the Pacific Islands Forum (PIF), and the Indian Ocean Commission (IOC) facilitate regional cooperation on issues such as climate change adaptation, fisheries management, and disaster risk reduction, fostering regional solidarity and collective action in SIDS.

8. Knowledge Networks and Platforms:

Knowledge networks and platforms serve as mechanisms for sharing information, best practices, and lessons learned among SIDS and their international partners. Platforms such as the SIDS Partnership Framework, the Global Island Partnership (GLISPA), and the International Seabed Authority (ISA) provide forums for dialogue, collaboration, and knowledge exchange on sustainable development priorities and initiatives in SIDS.

In summary, international cooperation and partnerships are essential for supporting Small Island Developing States (SIDS) in addressing their unique development challenges and advancing sustainable development agendas. By fostering collaboration, mobilizing resources, and promoting knowledge exchange, international partners and stakeholders can empower SIDS to build resilience, achieve sustainable development goals, and create a more equitable and sustainable future for all.

In conclusion, effective governance, sound policy frameworks, and meaningful partnerships are critical for advancing sustainable development in Small Island Developing States. By strengthening institutional capacity, crafting integrated policy frameworks, engaging civil society and communities, and fostering international cooperation and partnerships, SIDS can overcome challenges, seize opportunities, and achieve their sustainable development aspirations.

Chapter – 11

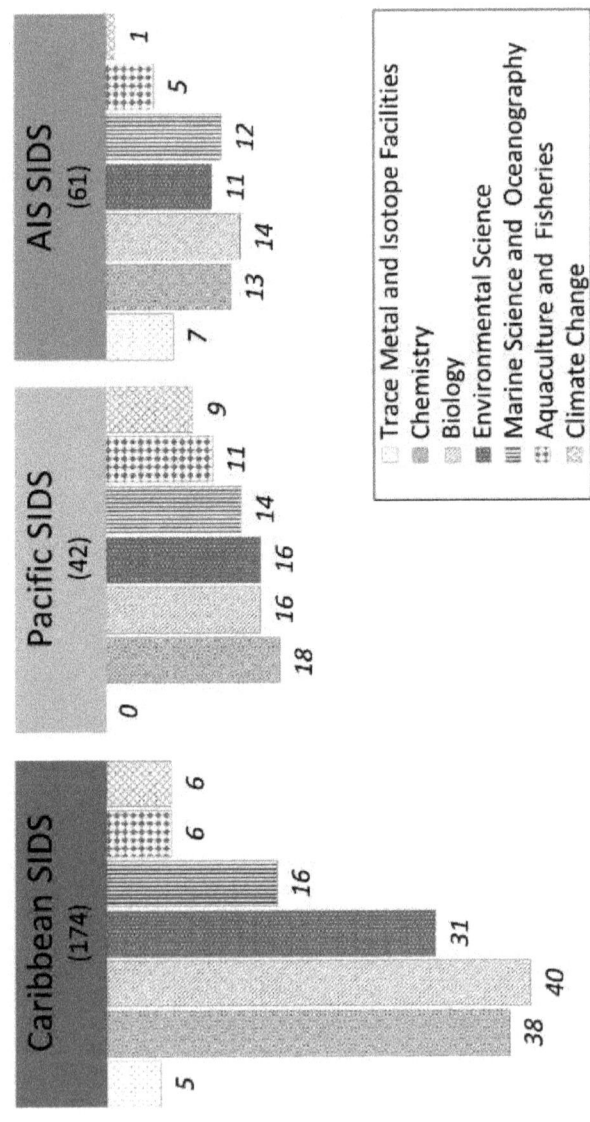

Education, Awareness, and Capacity Building

Education, awareness, and capacity building are fundamental pillars for promoting sustainable development in Small Island Developing States (SIDS). This chapter explores the importance of education for sustainable development, raising awareness on environmental issues, building local capacity, and integrating sustainability into curriculum and training programs.

11.1 Importance of Education for Sustainable Development

Education plays a pivotal role in fostering awareness, promoting behavioral change, and building the capacity of individuals and communities to address the complex challenges of sustainable development. This section explores the significance of education for sustainable development (ESD), its transformative potential, and strategies for integrating sustainability principles into educational systems in Small Island Developing States (SIDS).

1. **Empowering Individuals and Communities:**
Education empowers individuals and communities with the knowledge, skills, and attitudes needed to understand, appreciate, and actively engage in sustainable development initiatives. By raising awareness of environmental, social, and economic issues, education equips individuals with the tools to make informed decisions, adopt sustainable lifestyles, and advocate for positive change in SIDS.

2. **Promoting Environmental Stewardship:**
Education fosters environmental stewardship by instilling values of respect, responsibility, and care for the natural environment. Through environmental education programs, students learn about ecosystems, biodiversity, and the importance of conservation, inspiring them to become stewards of the environment and protectors of fragile ecosystems in SIDS.

3. **Building Resilience to Climate Change:**
Education enhances resilience to climate change by promoting climate literacy, disaster preparedness, and adaptive capacity among individuals and communities in SIDS. Through climate change education initiatives, students learn about the impacts of climate change, adaptation strategies, and mitigation measures, enabling

them to take proactive measures to mitigate risks and build climate-resilient communities.

4. Fostering Sustainable Lifestyles and Consumption Patterns:

Education promotes sustainable lifestyles and consumption patterns by raising awareness of the social, economic, and environmental consequences of unsustainable practices. By integrating sustainability principles into curricula, education encourages students to adopt behaviors that minimize resource consumption, reduce waste generation, and promote sustainable consumption and production patterns in SIDS.

5. Cultivating Critical Thinking and Problem-Solving Skills:

Education cultivates critical thinking and problem-solving skills essential for addressing complex sustainability challenges in SIDS. Through inquiry-based learning, experiential education, and participatory approaches, students develop analytical skills, creativity, and innovative solutions to real-world sustainability issues, empowering them to become agents of change in their communities.

6. Promoting Social Equity and Inclusion:

Education promotes social equity and inclusion by providing equitable access to quality education and opportunities for all individuals, regardless of gender, ethnicity, or socio-economic background. By addressing barriers to education, promoting gender equality, and fostering inclusive learning environments, education contributes to social cohesion, empowerment, and poverty reduction in SIDS.

7. Strengthening Institutional Capacity and Governance:

Education strengthens institutional capacity and governance by building the skills, knowledge, and expertise of educators, policymakers, and other stakeholders to integrate sustainability principles into educational systems and policies in SIDS. Through professional development programs, curriculum reforms, and institutional partnerships, education enhances the capacity of educational institutions to promote sustainable development and advance national development agendas in SIDS.

8. Fostering Lifelong Learning and Continuous Improvement:

Education fosters lifelong learning and continuous improvement by instilling a culture of curiosity, inquiry, and self-reflection among individuals and communities in SIDS. By promoting lifelong learning opportunities, non-formal education initiatives, and community-based learning approaches, education enables individuals to adapt to changing circumstances, acquire new knowledge and skills, and contribute to sustainable development throughout their lives.

In summary, education for sustainable development (ESD) is essential for promoting awareness, fostering empowerment, and building resilience to address the complex challenges faced by Small Island Developing States (SIDS). By integrating sustainability principles into educational systems, fostering critical thinking, and promoting inclusive learning opportunities, education empowers individuals and communities to contribute to sustainable development, build resilient societies, and create a more equitable and sustainable future for all in SIDS.

11.2 Raising Awareness on Environmental Issues

Raising awareness on environmental issues is a crucial component of sustainable development efforts in Small Island Developing States (SIDS). This section delves into the importance of environmental awareness, strategies for raising awareness, and the role of awareness campaigns in promoting environmental conservation and sustainability in SIDS.

1. Importance of Environmental Awareness:

Environmental awareness is essential for fostering a deeper understanding of the interconnectedness between human activities and the natural environment in SIDS. By raising awareness of environmental issues such as climate change, biodiversity loss, and pollution, individuals and communities become empowered to take action to protect and preserve their natural resources and ecosystems.

2. Understanding Local Environmental Challenges:

Raising awareness involves educating individuals about the specific environmental challenges faced by their communities in SIDS. By understanding the local context, including vulnerabilities to climate change, threats to biodiversity, and issues related to waste management and pollution, communities can develop targeted solutions and strategies to address these challenges effectively.

3. Promoting Sustainable Lifestyles:

Environmental awareness campaigns promote sustainable lifestyles and behaviors that reduce ecological footprints and minimize negative impacts on the environment in SIDS. By advocating for practices such as energy conservation, waste reduction, sustainable transportation, and eco-friendly consumption, awareness initiatives empower individuals to make informed choices that contribute to environmental sustainability and resilience.

4. Engaging Stakeholders and Civil Society:

Raising awareness involves engaging stakeholders, including civil society organizations, local communities, and youth groups, as key partners in environmental conservation efforts in SIDS. By fostering collaboration, dialogue, and participation, awareness campaigns mobilize collective action, build social capital, and promote community ownership of environmental initiatives, leading to more inclusive and sustainable outcomes.

5. Leveraging Traditional Knowledge and Cultural Values:

Environmental awareness initiatives recognize the importance of traditional knowledge and cultural values in promoting environmental stewardship and resilience in SIDS. By integrating indigenous wisdom, local practices, and cultural values into awareness campaigns, communities reaffirm their connection to the land, foster a sense of responsibility towards nature, and promote sustainable management of natural resources.

6. Utilizing Information and Communication Technologies (ICTs):

Advancements in information and communication technologies (ICTs) offer innovative tools and platforms for raising awareness on environmental issues in SIDS. Through social media, websites, mobile applications, and online forums, awareness campaigns reach wider audiences, facilitate knowledge sharing, and promote dialogue and exchange of ideas on environmental conservation and sustainability.

7. Educating the Youth:

Raising awareness among the youth is critical for building a generation of environmentally conscious and responsible citizens in SIDS. By integrating environmental education into school curricula, extracurricular activities, and youth programs, awareness initiatives empower young people to become environmental advocates, change agents, and leaders in promoting sustainable development in their communities.

8. Monitoring and Evaluation of Awareness Campaigns:

Monitoring and evaluating awareness campaigns are essential for assessing their effectiveness, identifying areas for improvement, and measuring their impact on behavior change and environmental outcomes in SIDS. Through surveys, interviews, and feedback mechanisms, awareness initiatives gather data on knowledge, attitudes, and practices, informing strategic decision-making and enhancing the relevance and impact of future campaigns.

In summary, raising awareness on environmental issues is a fundamental component of sustainable development efforts in Small Island Developing States (SIDS). By promoting understanding, encouraging sustainable behaviors, and fostering collaboration among stakeholders, awareness campaigns empower individuals and communities to become active stewards of their environment, contributing to the conservation and sustainability of their natural resources and ecosystems in SIDS.

11.3 Building Local Capacity for Sustainable Development

Building local capacity is essential for empowering communities, enhancing resilience, and promoting sustainable development in Small Island Developing States (SIDS). This section explores the importance of building local capacity, strategies for capacity development, and the role of local actors in driving sustainable development initiatives in SIDS.

1. Importance of Local Capacity Building:

Building local capacity is critical for strengthening the ability of communities and institutions to address their development challenges and seize opportunities for sustainable development in SIDS. By enhancing skills, knowledge, and resources at the local level, capacity building fosters self-reliance, promotes innovation, and empowers communities to drive their own development agendas.

2. Strengthening Institutional Capacity:

Building institutional capacity involves enhancing the skills, systems, and structures of government agencies, civil society organizations, and other institutions to effectively plan, implement, and monitor sustainable development initiatives in SIDS. Through training programs, institutional reforms, and strategic investments, capacity building initiatives improve governance, promote transparency, and enhance service delivery in SIDS.

3. Promoting Community-Led Development:

Capacity building initiatives promote community-led development approaches that empower local communities to identify their needs, set priorities, and implement sustainable development projects in SIDS. By fostering participatory decision-making, building leadership skills, and providing technical support, capacity development efforts enable communities to take ownership of their development processes and create positive change from within.

4. Supporting Knowledge Transfer and Exchange:

Building local capacity involves facilitating knowledge transfer and exchange among stakeholders, including governments, civil society organizations, academia, and local communities, to promote learning and innovation in SIDS. Through knowledge sharing platforms, peer-to-peer networks, and experiential learning opportunities, capacity building initiatives leverage local expertise, best practices, and lessons learned to address development challenges and promote sustainable solutions in SIDS.

5. Enhancing Technical and Vocational Skills:

Capacity building initiatives focus on enhancing technical and vocational skills relevant to sustainable development priorities, such as renewable energy, sustainable agriculture, and climate resilience, to meet the evolving needs of SIDS. By providing training, apprenticeships, and certification programs, capacity development efforts equip individuals with the practical skills and competencies needed to access employment opportunities, support local industries, and contribute to sustainable development efforts in SIDS.

6. Fostering Collaboration and Partnerships:

Building local capacity involves fostering collaboration and partnerships among stakeholders, including government agencies, civil society organizations, private sector entities, and local communities, to pool resources, share expertise, and leverage synergies for sustainable development in SIDS. Through joint initiatives, multi-stakeholder platforms, and public-private partnerships, capacity building efforts promote collective action, enhance coordination, and maximize impact in addressing development challenges in SIDS.

7. Investing in Education and Training:

Capacity building initiatives invest in education and training programs that equip individuals with the knowledge, skills, and attitudes needed to address sustainable development challenges in SIDS. By supporting formal and non-formal education initiatives, vocational training programs, and lifelong learning opportunities, capacity development efforts empower individuals to become active participants in sustainable development initiatives and agents of positive change in their communities.

8. Mainstreaming Gender and Social Inclusion:

Building local capacity involves mainstreaming gender and social inclusion considerations into capacity development initiatives to ensure that marginalized groups, including women, youth, indigenous peoples, and persons with disabilities, are actively engaged in decision-making processes and benefit from sustainable development efforts in SIDS. By promoting gender-responsive and inclusive approaches, capacity building efforts enhance equity, diversity, and social cohesion in SIDS.

In summary, building local capacity is essential for promoting sustainable development, enhancing resilience, and empowering communities in Small Island Developing States (SIDS). By strengthening institutional capacity, supporting community-led development, and investing in education and training, capacity building initiatives enable local actors to drive sustainable development agendas, build resilient societies, and create a more equitable and sustainable future for all in SIDS.

11.4 Integrating Sustainability into Curriculum and Training Programs

Integrating sustainability into curriculum and training programs is a key strategy for promoting education for sustainable development (ESD) and building the capacity of individuals and institutions to address sustainable development challenges in Small Island Developing States (SIDS). This section explores the importance of integrating sustainability into education and training, approaches for curriculum development, and examples of successful initiatives in SIDS.

1. Importance of Integrating Sustainability:

Integrating sustainability into curriculum and training programs is essential for equipping learners with the knowledge, skills, and values needed to understand and address complex sustainability challenges in SIDS. By incorporating sustainability principles across disciplines, educational institutions prepare students to become informed global citizens, critical thinkers, and agents of positive change in their communities.

2. Holistic Approach to Curriculum Development:

Curriculum development involves adopting a holistic approach that integrates sustainability principles into all aspects of teaching and learning in SIDS. By embedding sustainability concepts, themes, and case studies into curriculum frameworks, learning outcomes, and assessment practices, educational institutions promote interdisciplinary learning, foster systems thinking, and cultivate a deeper understanding of sustainability issues among students.

3. Experiential and Inquiry-Based Learning:

Integrating sustainability into curriculum and training programs involves adopting experiential and inquiry-based learning approaches that engage students in real-world sustainability challenges and solutions in SIDS. By providing hands-on experiences, field trips, and project-based learning opportunities, educational institutions foster critical thinking, creativity, and problem-solving skills among students, enabling them to apply theory to practice and make meaningful contributions to sustainable development initiatives.

4. Cross-Curricular and Interdisciplinary Perspectives:

Integrating sustainability into curriculum and training programs involves promoting cross-curricular and interdisciplinary perspectives that explore the interconnectedness of social, economic, and environmental issues in SIDS. By fostering collaboration among different disciplines, such as science, social studies, and the arts, educational institutions enable students to gain a holistic understanding of sustainability challenges and develop integrated solutions that address multiple dimensions of sustainability.

5. Indigenous Knowledge and Local Context:

Integrating sustainability into curriculum and training programs involves recognizing and incorporating indigenous knowledge, local practices, and cultural values that contribute to sustainable development in SIDS. By valuing traditional wisdom, respecting cultural diversity, and incorporating local examples and case studies into curriculum materials, educational institutions promote relevance, authenticity, and inclusivity in sustainability education initiatives.

6. Professional Development and Teacher Training:

Integrating sustainability into curriculum and training programs involves providing professional development and teacher training opportunities that enhance educators' capacity to teach and integrate sustainability concepts into their classrooms in SIDS. By offering workshops, seminars, and training courses on ESD pedagogy, curriculum design, and assessment strategies, educational institutions empower educators to become effective facilitators of sustainability education and advocates for change in SIDS.

7. Partnerships and Stakeholder Engagement:

Integrating sustainability into curriculum and training programs involves forging partnerships and engaging stakeholders, including government agencies, civil society organizations, and the private sector, to support curriculum development and implementation efforts in SIDS. By collaborating with external partners, sharing resources, and leveraging expertise, educational institutions enhance the relevance, impact, and sustainability of sustainability education initiatives in SIDS.

8. Monitoring and Evaluation of Impact:

Integrating sustainability into curriculum and training programs involves monitoring and evaluating the impact of sustainability education initiatives on student learning outcomes, behavior change, and societal impact in SIDS. By collecting data, conducting assessments, and soliciting feedback from stakeholders, educational institutions measure the effectiveness of curriculum integration efforts, identify areas for improvement, and inform future curriculum development and implementation strategies in SIDS.

In summary, integrating sustainability into curriculum and training programs is essential for promoting education for sustainable development (ESD) and building the capacity of individuals and institutions to address sustainable development challenges in Small Island Developing States (SIDS). By adopting a holistic approach to curriculum development, fostering experiential and inquiry-based learning, and engaging stakeholders, educational institutions prepare students to become active agents of positive change and contribute to building a more sustainable future for all in SIDS.

In conclusion, education, awareness, and capacity building are essential enablers for advancing sustainable development in Small Island Developing States. By investing in education for sustainable development, raising awareness on environmental issues, building local capacity, and integrating sustainability into curriculum and training programs, SIDS can empower individuals, communities, and institutions to contribute effectively to a more sustainable and resilient future.

Chapter – 12

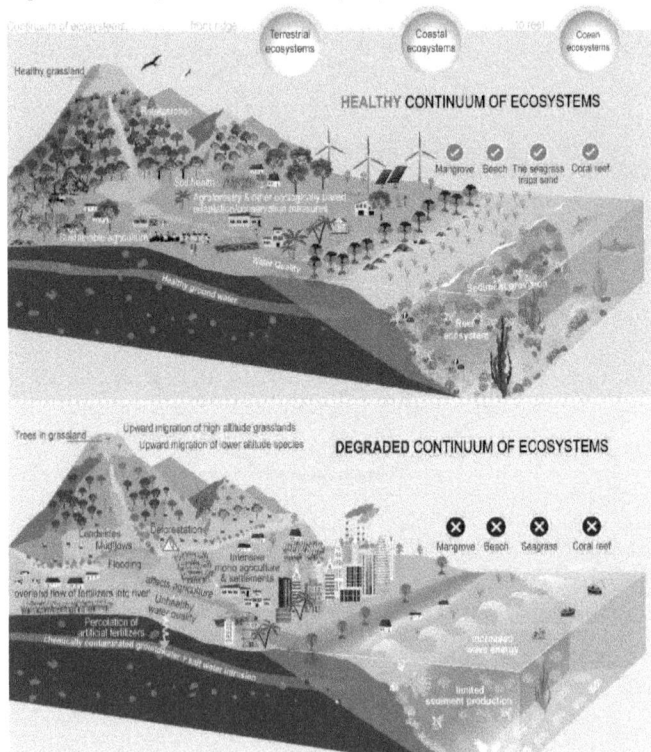

Ridge-to-reef interrelated protection services delivered by ecosystems on small islands

Conclusion and Future Perspectives

As Small Island Developing States (SIDS) navigate the complexities of sustainable development, reflecting on achievements, challenges, and future prospects is essential. This concluding chapter examines the progress made, ongoing challenges, the role of technology, and outlines a vision for a sustainable future for SIDS, emphasizing the importance of collective action and community empowerment.

12.1 Achievements and Remaining Challenges

SIDS have made significant strides in advancing sustainable development, including:

- **Environmental Conservation:** SIDS have implemented conservation efforts, protected marine and terrestrial ecosystems, and promoted sustainable resource management practices.

- **Climate Resilience:** SIDS have developed adaptation strategies, enhanced disaster preparedness, and advocated for climate action on the global stage.

- **Renewable Energy:** SIDS have invested in renewable energy infrastructure, reduced reliance on fossil fuels, and promoted energy efficiency measures.

- **Community Empowerment:** SIDS have engaged communities, fostered local capacity building, and promoted social inclusion and equity in development initiatives.

However, significant challenges remain, including:

- **Climate Change Impacts:** SIDS continue to face the disproportionate impacts of climate change, including sea-level rise, extreme weather events, and coastal erosion.

- **Environmental Degradation:** SIDS struggle with environmental degradation, loss of biodiversity, pollution, and unsustainable land use practices.

- **Economic Vulnerability:** SIDS grapple with economic vulnerability, dependence on limited resources, vulnerability to external shocks, and economic disparities.

- **Social Inequities:** SIDS confront social inequities, including poverty, inequality, health disparities, and lack of access to basic services and opportunities.

Addressing these challenges requires sustained commitment, innovative solutions, and collaborative efforts from all stakeholders.

In the journey towards sustainable development in Small Island Developing States (SIDS), significant achievements have been made, yet numerous challenges persist. This section evaluates the accomplishments attained thus far and identifies the remaining hurdles hindering the progress towards sustainable development goals in SIDS.

1. Achievements:

- *International Recognition:* SIDS have garnered international recognition for their unique vulnerabilities and contributions to global sustainable development agendas. Through platforms like the United Nations, SIDS have successfully advocated for their specific needs and challenges to be addressed on the global stage.

- *Policy Development:* SIDS have developed and implemented various policy frameworks and strategies to address sustainable development challenges. Initiatives such as the SAMOA Pathway, regional action plans, and national sustainable development strategies demonstrate the commitment of SIDS to prioritize sustainable development goals.

- *Environmental Conservation:* SIDS have made significant strides in environmental conservation, including the establishment of marine protected areas, conservation efforts for endangered species, and initiatives to promote renewable energy and sustainable resource management practices.

- *Community Empowerment:* SIDS have empowered local communities to participate in sustainable development initiatives, fostering a sense of ownership, resilience, and innovation. Through community-based projects, education programs, and partnerships, SIDS have built social capital and strengthened grassroots movements for sustainable development.

- *International Cooperation:* SIDS have engaged in international cooperation and partnerships to address common challenges and leverage resources and expertise from the global community. Collaborative initiatives with international organizations, donor agencies, and development partners have facilitated knowledge exchange, capacity building, and resource mobilization for sustainable development in SIDS.

2. Remaining Challenges:

- *Climate Change Vulnerability:* SIDS remain highly vulnerable to the impacts of climate change, including sea-level rise, extreme weather events, and coastal erosion. Limited resources, inadequate infrastructure, and institutional capacity constraints exacerbate the challenges faced by SIDS in adapting to and mitigating the effects of climate change.

- *Environmental Degradation:* SIDS continue to experience environmental degradation, including deforestation, loss of biodiversity, and pollution of air, land, and water resources. Unsustainable land use practices, overexploitation of natural resources, and inadequate waste management systems pose significant threats to the ecological integrity of SIDS.

- *Economic Vulnerability:* SIDS grapple with economic vulnerabilities, including high dependence on a few key industries such as tourism and agriculture, limited access to finance and investment opportunities, and susceptibility to external shocks such as economic downturns and natural disasters.

- *Social Inequities:* SIDS face persistent social inequities, including poverty, inequality, and marginalization of vulnerable groups such as women, youth, and indigenous populations. Limited access to education, healthcare, and basic services exacerbates social disparities and undermines efforts to achieve inclusive and equitable development in SIDS.

- *Governance Challenges:* SIDS confront governance challenges, including weak institutions, corruption, and political instability, which impede effective policy implementation and hinder progress towards sustainable development goals. Strengthening governance mechanisms, promoting transparency, and fostering accountability are critical for addressing governance challenges in SIDS.

3. Path Forward:

Addressing the remaining challenges facing SIDS requires sustained commitment, collaboration, and innovation from all stakeholders. Efforts to strengthen resilience, promote sustainable development, and achieve the Sustainable Development Goals must be prioritized at the local, regional, and international levels. Building on past achievements, SIDS must continue to leverage partnerships, mobilize resources, and implement transformative initiatives that promote inclusive, resilient, and sustainable development pathways for present and future generations. By addressing the remaining challenges with determination and resolve, SIDS can pave the way towards a more prosperous, equitable, and sustainable future for all.

12.2 The Role of Technology in Advancing Sustainable Development

Technology plays a pivotal role in advancing sustainable development goals by providing innovative solutions to address complex challenges faced by Small Island Developing States (SIDS). This section explores the diverse ways in which technology contributes to sustainable development efforts in SIDS, identifies key areas of technological innovation, and highlights the opportunities and challenges associated with the adoption of technology in advancing sustainability.

1. Enhancing Resource Efficiency:

Technology enables SIDS to improve resource efficiency by optimizing the use of natural resources, reducing waste generation, and minimizing environmental impacts. Innovations such as smart grids, energy-efficient appliances, and water-saving technologies help SIDS manage their limited resources more sustainably and enhance their resilience to climate change and environmental degradation.

2. Promoting Renewable Energy Deployment:

Technology plays a crucial role in promoting the deployment of renewable energy sources such as solar, wind, and hydroelectric power in SIDS. Advances in solar photovoltaic systems, wind turbines, and energy storage technologies have made renewable energy more accessible, affordable, and reliable, enabling SIDS to transition towards cleaner and more sustainable energy systems and reduce their dependence on imported fossil fuels.

3. Enhancing Climate Resilience:

Technology contributes to enhancing climate resilience in SIDS by providing early warning systems, climate modeling tools, and disaster risk management platforms to anticipate and mitigate the impacts of climate change-related hazards such as hurricanes, floods, and droughts. Remote sensing technologies, geographic information systems (GIS), and satellite imagery enable SIDS to monitor environmental changes, assess vulnerability, and develop adaptive strategies to build resilience and reduce disaster risks.

4. Improving Access to Education and Healthcare:

Technology improves access to education and healthcare services in SIDS by providing e-learning platforms, telemedicine solutions, and mobile health applications that enable remote communities to access quality education and healthcare services. Distance learning programs, virtual classrooms, and online medical consultations bridge geographical barriers, enhance access to information and expertise, and empower individuals to pursue lifelong learning and better health outcomes in SIDS.

5. Facilitating Sustainable Agriculture and Food Security:

Technology facilitates sustainable agriculture and food security in SIDS by providing precision farming technologies, climate-smart agricultural practices, and agrotechnology innovations that increase agricultural productivity, conserve natural resources, and improve food supply chains. Hydroponic systems, vertical farming, and agricultural drones enable SIDS to produce nutritious food in resource-constrained environments, enhance food security, and promote sustainable livelihoods for farmers and rural communities.

6. Fostering Innovation and Entrepreneurship:

Technology fosters innovation and entrepreneurship in SIDS by providing digital platforms, incubation centers, and startup ecosystems that support the development and scaling of sustainable business ventures. Digital payment systems, e-commerce platforms, and blockchain technology facilitate financial inclusion, access to markets, and economic diversification, driving economic growth, job creation, and poverty reduction in SIDS.

7. Promoting Environmental Monitoring and Conservation:

Technology promotes environmental monitoring and conservation in SIDS by providing remote sensing technologies, environmental sensors, and data analytics tools that enable real-time monitoring of ecosystems, biodiversity, and natural resources. Geographic information systems (GIS), satellite imagery, and citizen science initiatives empower local communities and conservation organizations to monitor environmental changes, track biodiversity, and implement targeted conservation interventions to protect fragile ecosystems and endangered species in SIDS.

8. Addressing Digital Divide and Technological Challenges:

Despite the opportunities offered by technology, SIDS face challenges related to the digital divide, inadequate infrastructure, and limited technical capacity that hinder the equitable access and effective utilization of technology for sustainable development. Addressing these challenges requires investment in ICT infrastructure, capacity building initiatives, and policy reforms to bridge the digital divide, promote digital literacy, and harness the full potential of technology for sustainable development in SIDS.

In summary, technology plays a transformative role in advancing sustainable development goals in Small Island Developing States (SIDS) by providing innovative solutions to address environmental, social, and economic challenges. By leveraging technology, SIDS can enhance resource efficiency, promote renewable energy deployment, build climate resilience, improve access to education and healthcare, foster innovation and entrepreneurship, and promote environmental monitoring and conservation. However, addressing technological challenges and ensuring equitable access to technology are essential for harnessing the full potential of technology to drive sustainable development in SIDS and create a more resilient, inclusive, and sustainable future for all.

12.3 Looking Ahead: Towards a Sustainable Future for SIDS

Looking ahead, SIDS envision a future characterized by:

- **Resilience:** SIDS aspire to build resilience to climate change, natural disasters, and socio-economic challenges, fostering adaptive capacity and sustainable livelihoods for their populations.

- **Sustainability:** SIDS are committed to promoting environmental sustainability, conservation of biodiversity, and sustainable use of natural resources, ensuring the well-being of current and future generations.

- **Inclusivity:** SIDS prioritize social inclusion, equity, and human rights, empowering marginalized groups, indigenous peoples, and women to participate fully in decision-making processes and benefit from development outcomes.

- **Innovation:** SIDS embrace innovation, technology, and entrepreneurship as drivers of sustainable development, fostering creativity, job creation, and economic diversification in key sectors.

- **Global Solidarity:** SIDS advocate for global solidarity, cooperation, and partnership in addressing common challenges, advocating for their unique vulnerabilities and contributions to sustainable development on the international stage.

By embracing these principles and working together towards a common vision, SIDS can achieve a sustainable and prosperous future for their citizens and the planet.

As Small Island Developing States (SIDS) navigate the complex challenges of sustainable development, it is crucial to envision a future that is resilient, inclusive, and sustainable. This section explores the pathways towards a sustainable future for SIDS, identifies key priorities and strategies, and underscores the importance of collective action and partnership in shaping a brighter tomorrow.

1. Embracing Sustainable Development Goals:

SIDS must continue to prioritize the implementation of the Sustainable Development Goals (SDGs) to address the interconnected challenges of poverty eradication, environmental conservation, and social inclusion. By aligning national development agendas with the SDGs, SIDS can mobilize resources, foster collaboration, and accelerate progress towards achieving the 2030 Agenda for Sustainable Development.

2. Building Climate Resilience:

Climate change poses a significant threat to the livelihoods, ecosystems, and economies of SIDS. Building climate resilience requires investing in adaptation measures, disaster risk reduction strategies, and sustainable infrastructure to mitigate the impacts of extreme weather events, sea-level rise, and coastal erosion. By mainstreaming climate resilience into development planning and promoting nature-based solutions, SIDS can enhance their adaptive capacity and build more resilient communities and economies.

3. Promoting Renewable Energy and Energy Efficiency:

Transitioning towards renewable energy sources and improving energy efficiency is essential for reducing greenhouse gas emissions, enhancing energy security, and promoting sustainable development in SIDS. By investing in renewable energy infrastructure, promoting energy conservation measures, and adopting clean energy technologies, SIDS can diversify their energy mix, reduce dependence on imported fossil fuels, and promote sustainable energy systems that support economic growth and environmental sustainability.

4. Strengthening Environmental Conservation and Biodiversity Protection:

Protecting natural ecosystems, conserving biodiversity, and promoting sustainable natural resource management are essential for safeguarding the ecological integrity and resilience of SIDS. By establishing protected areas, implementing conservation strategies, and engaging local communities in ecosystem stewardship, SIDS can preserve their unique biodiversity, mitigate habitat loss, and promote sustainable livelihoods that support both people and nature.

5. Enhancing Social Inclusion and Equity:

Promoting social inclusion, gender equality, and equitable access to opportunities are fundamental principles for advancing sustainable development in SIDS. By addressing social disparities, empowering marginalized groups, and promoting inclusive policies and programs, SIDS can build more resilient and cohesive societies that leave no one behind and ensure that all individuals have the opportunity to thrive and prosper.

6. Fostering Innovation and Entrepreneurship:

Harnessing the power of innovation and entrepreneurship is essential for driving sustainable development and economic diversification in SIDS. By investing in research and development, supporting startup ecosystems, and fostering a culture of innovation and creativity, SIDS can unlock new opportunities, create sustainable livelihoods, and promote economic resilience in a rapidly changing world.

7. Strengthening Governance and Partnerships:

Effective governance mechanisms, transparent institutions, and multi-stakeholder partnerships are essential for advancing sustainable development goals in SIDS. By promoting good governance practices, enhancing accountability, and fostering collaboration among governments, civil society, the private sector, and international organizations, SIDS can leverage collective expertise, resources, and political will to address shared challenges and achieve common objectives.

8. Empowering Communities and Stakeholders:

Empowering communities and stakeholders to participate in decision-making processes, advocate for their rights, and contribute to sustainable development initiatives is essential for building ownership, resilience, and sustainability in SIDS. By promoting participatory approaches, fostering dialogue, and strengthening local capacities, SIDS can tap into the knowledge, creativity, and resilience of their people to co-create solutions that address their unique challenges and aspirations.

In summary, the journey towards a sustainable future for Small Island Developing States (SIDS) requires concerted efforts, visionary leadership, and collective action from all stakeholders. By embracing the Sustainable Development Goals, building climate resilience, promoting renewable energy and energy efficiency, strengthening environmental conservation, enhancing social inclusion and equity, fostering innovation and entrepreneurship, strengthening governance and partnerships, and empowering communities and stakeholders, SIDS can chart a course towards a more resilient, inclusive, and sustainable future for present and future generations

12.4 Call to Action: Empowering Communities and Stakeholders

A call to action is issued to empower communities and stakeholders in advancing sustainable development in SIDS:

- **Governments:** Governments are urged to prioritize sustainable development in policy-making, planning, and resource allocation, fostering political will, institutional capacity, and good governance for sustainable outcomes.

- **Civil Society:** Civil society organizations, NGOs, and community-based groups are encouraged to mobilize grassroots action, raise awareness, and advocate for policy reforms that promote environmental sustainability, social equity, and economic resilience.

- **Private Sector:** The private sector is called upon to invest in sustainable business practices, innovation, and corporate social responsibility, aligning business objectives with sustainable development goals and contributing to positive social and environmental outcomes.

- **International Community:** The international community is urged to support SIDS through financial assistance, technology transfer, capacity building, and partnerships, honoring commitments under global agreements such as the Paris Agreement, the Sendai Framework, and the Sustainable Development Goals.

By fostering collaboration, solidarity, and shared responsibility, stakeholders can create a more inclusive, resilient, and sustainable future for SIDS and the global community.

Empowering communities and stakeholders is essential for driving sustainable development initiatives in Small Island Developing States (SIDS). This section issues a call to action, urging governments, civil society organizations, the private sector, and international partners to collaborate and prioritize efforts to empower communities and stakeholders in SIDS.

1. Strengthening Community Participation:

Governments and organizations must prioritize efforts to strengthen community participation in decision-making processes related to sustainable development. By fostering inclusive and participatory approaches, such as community consultations, participatory planning, and citizen engagement mechanisms, stakeholders can ensure that local voices are heard, priorities are addressed, and solutions are tailored to the needs of communities in SIDS.

2. Investing in Education and Capacity Building:

Investing in education and capacity building initiatives is crucial for empowering individuals and communities to actively participate in sustainable development efforts. Governments and organizations should prioritize investments in education, vocational training, and lifelong learning programs that equip people with the knowledge, skills, and tools needed to address sustainable development challenges, promote innovation, and build resilience in SIDS.

3. Promoting Gender Equality and Social Inclusion:

Promoting gender equality and social inclusion is essential for ensuring that all members of society have equal opportunities to participate in and benefit from sustainable development initiatives. Governments and organizations must adopt policies and programs that promote women's empowerment, protect the rights of marginalized groups, and address social disparities to create more inclusive and equitable societies in SIDS.

4. Fostering Multi-Stakeholder Partnerships:

Fostering multi-stakeholder partnerships is critical for leveraging collective expertise, resources, and networks to address complex sustainable development challenges in SIDS. Governments, civil society organizations, the private sector, and international partners should collaborate to create enabling environments for dialogue, cooperation, and joint action, and promote synergy and alignment of efforts towards common goals in SIDS.

5. Supporting Grassroots Initiatives and Innovations:

Supporting grassroots initiatives and innovations is key to unlocking the creativity, resilience, and potential of local communities in driving sustainable development in SIDS. Governments and organizations should provide support, resources, and recognition to grassroots organizations, social entrepreneurs, and community-led initiatives that are advancing innovative solutions to address local challenges and promote sustainable development at the grassroots level.

6. Strengthening Governance and Accountability:

Strengthening governance and accountability mechanisms is essential for ensuring transparency, integrity, and effectiveness in sustainable development initiatives in SIDS. Governments and organizations should promote good governance practices, enhance accountability mechanisms, and foster transparency in decision-making processes to build trust, promote public confidence, and ensure the effective implementation of sustainable development policies and programs in SIDS.

7. Mobilizing Resources and Investments:

Mobilizing resources and investments is critical for scaling up sustainable development efforts in SIDS and achieving the Sustainable Development Goals. Governments, international organizations, and development partners should prioritize investments in sustainable development projects and initiatives that empower communities, promote resilience, and create long-term positive impacts on people and the planet in SIDS.

8. Amplifying Voices on the Global Stage:

Amplifying the voices of SIDS on the global stage is essential for advocating for their specific needs, priorities, and challenges in international forums and decision-making processes. Governments, civil society organizations, and international partners should support efforts to raise awareness, build alliances, and advocate for policy reforms that address the unique vulnerabilities and aspirations of SIDS and promote their sustainable development agenda on the global agenda.

In conclusion, empowering communities and stakeholders is a fundamental prerequisite for driving sustainable development initiatives in Small Island Developing States (SIDS). By strengthening community participation, investing in education and capacity building, promoting gender equality and social inclusion, fostering multi-stakeholder partnerships, supporting grassroots initiatives and innovations, strengthening governance and accountability, mobilizing resources and investments, and amplifying voices on the global stage, stakeholders can work together to empower communities, build resilience, and create a more sustainable and equitable future for all in SIDS.

In conclusion, while Small Island Developing States face numerous challenges on their path to sustainable development, they also possess resilience, creativity, and determination to overcome obstacles and achieve their aspirations. By leveraging their strengths, embracing innovation, and fostering partnerships, SIDS can chart a course towards a sustainable future that ensures the well-being of their people and the preservation of their unique natural and cultural heritage.

Dr. Chirag Bhimani

List of Acronyms

Abbreviations & Acronyms

- **SIDS** - Small Island Developing States
- **IWRM** - Integrated Water Resource Management
- **CSOs** - Civil Society Organizations
- **NGOs** - Non-Governmental Organizations
- **CBOs** - Community-Based Organizations
- **ESD** - Education for Sustainable Development
- **ODA** - Official Development Assistance
- **SAMOA** - Small Island Developing States Accelerated Modalities of Action
- **SDGs** - Sustainable Development Goals
- **ESG** - Environmental, Social, and Governance
- **IPM** - Integrated Pest Management
- **AOSIS** - Alliance of Small Island States
- **ICT** - Information and Communication Technology
- **EIA** - Environmental Impact Assessment
- **GDP** - Gross Domestic Product
- **UN** - United Nations
- **COP** - Conference of the Parties
- **GEF** - Global Environment Facility

> **UNEP -** United Nations Environment Program me

> **UNESCO** - United Nations Educational, Scientific and Cultural Organization

This list provides a reference for readers to quickly understand and identify key terms and concepts mentioned throughout the book "Sustaining Paradise: Sustainable Development in Small Island Developing States (SIDS)."

Glossary of Terms

> **Biodiversity:** The variety of life forms, including species diversity, genetic diversity, and ecosystem diversity, within a given ecosystem, region, or planet.

> **Climate Resilience:** The ability of communities, ecosystems, and socio-economic systems to withstand, adapt to, and recover from the impacts of climate change, including extreme weather events, sea-level rise, and shifting climatic conditions.

> **Ecosystem Services:** The benefits provided by ecosystems to human well-being, including provisioning services (such as food, water, and raw materials), regulating services (such as climate regulation, flood control, and pollination), cultural services (such as recreational and aesthetic value), and supporting services (such as nutrient cycling and soil formation).

> **Green Economy:** An economy that aims to promote sustainable development by fostering economic growth, social inclusion, and environmental sustainability, through investments in clean technologies, renewable energy, resource efficiency, and green infrastructure.

- ➢ **Indigenous Knowledge:** Traditional knowledge, practices, and wisdom passed down through generations by indigenous peoples, relating to natural resource management, environmental conservation, and cultural heritage.

- ➢ **Ocean Acidification:** The ongoing decrease in the pH of the Earth's oceans, primarily caused by the absorption of carbon dioxide (CO_2) from the atmosphere, which leads to changes in marine chemistry and poses risks to marine ecosystems, including coral reefs and shellfish populations.

- ➢ **Sustainable Development:** Development that meets the needs of the present without compromising the ability of future generations to meet their own needs, integrating economic, social, and environmental dimensions to promote well-being and prosperity for all.

- ➢ **Vulnerability:** The degree to which a system, community, or population is susceptible to harm, damage, or disruption from external stressors, including environmental hazards, socio-economic disparities, and institutional weaknesses.

- ➤ **Water Scarcity:** A condition where the demand for water exceeds the available supply, leading to inadequate access to safe drinking water, reduced agricultural productivity, and environmental degradation.

- ➤ **Zero Waste:** A waste management approach that aims to minimize the generation of waste, maximize resource recovery, and eliminate the disposal of materials into landfills or incineration, through strategies such as recycling, composting, and waste reduction.

This glossary provides definitions for key terms and concepts related to sustainable development in Small Island Developing States (SIDS), aiding readers in understanding the content and terminology used throughout the book "Sustaining Paradise: Sustainable Development in Small Island Developing States (SIDS)."

Resources and Further Reading

1. **United Nations Development Programme (UNDP) - Small Island Developing States:** Visit the UNDP website for comprehensive information, reports, and resources on sustainable development in Small Island Developing States (SIDS). [UNDP SIDS](https://www.undp.org/content/undp/en/home/librarypage/sustainable-development-goals/sids.html)

2. **Alliance of Small Island States (AOSIS):** Explore the official website of AOSIS to access policy briefs, statements, and publications advocating for the interests and concerns of small island nations in international forums. [AOSIS](https://www.aosis.org/)

3. **Small Island Developing States Network (SIDSNet):** Access the SIDSNet platform, hosted by the United Nations Office of the High Representative for the Least Developed Countries, Landlocked Developing Countries, and Small Island Developing States (UN-OHRLLS), for news, events, and resources on sustainable development in SIDS. [SIDSNet](https://sidsnet.org/)

4. **World Bank - Small States Hub:** Visit the World Bank's Small States Hub for data, reports, and projects addressing the unique challenges and opportunities faced by small island nations in achieving sustainable development. [World Bank Small States Hub](https://www.worldbank.org/en/country/smallstates)

5. **United Nations Environment Programme (UNEP) - SIDS Portfolio:** Explore UNEP's portfolio of initiatives and resources aimed at supporting environmental conservation, climate resilience, and sustainable development in Small Island Developing States. [UNEP SIDS Portfolio](https://www.unep.org/topics/sids)

6. **Sustainable Development Goals (SDGs):** Learn more about the 17 Sustainable Development Goals and their targets, indicators, and progress towards achieving sustainable development worldwide. [United Nations SDGs](https://sdgs.un.org/)

7. **Intergovernmental Panel on Climate Change (IPCC) - Special Report on the Ocean and Cryosphere in a Changing Climate:** Access the IPCC's special report on the impacts of climate

change on the ocean and cryosphere, including implications for Small Island Developing States. [IPCC Special Report](https://www.ipcc.ch/srocc/)

8. **The SAMOA Pathway:** Read the outcome document of the Third International Conference on Small Island Developing States (SIDS), known as the SAMOA Pathway, which outlines priority areas for action and international support for sustainable development in SIDS. [SAMOA Pathway](https://sustainabledevelopment.un.org/sids/samoapathway)

9. **Sustainable Energy for All (SEforALL):** Explore SEforALL's resources, reports, and initiatives aimed at promoting access to clean and affordable energy for all, including efforts to support sustainable energy transitions in Small Island Developing States. [SEforALL](https://www.seforall.org/)

10. **Pacific Islands Forum Secretariat:** Visit the official website of the Pacific Islands Forum Secretariat for news, publications, and regional initiatives addressing sustainable development, climate change, and regional cooperation among

Pacific Island countries and territories. [Pacific Islands Forum](https://www.forumsec.org/)

These resources provide valuable information, research, and guidance for policymakers, practitioners, researchers, and stakeholders interested in sustainable development in Small Island Developing States (SIDS), complementing the content of the book "Sustaining Paradise: Sustainable Development in Small Island Developing States (SIDS)."

www.ingramcontent.com/pod-product-compliance
Lightning Source LLC
LaVergne TN
LVHW061608070526
838199LV00078B/7207